SUPREME COURT JUSTICES

# JOHN
# MARSHALL

SUPREME COURT JUSTICES
# JOHN
# MARSHALL

Jim Corrigan

**Greensboro, North Carolina**

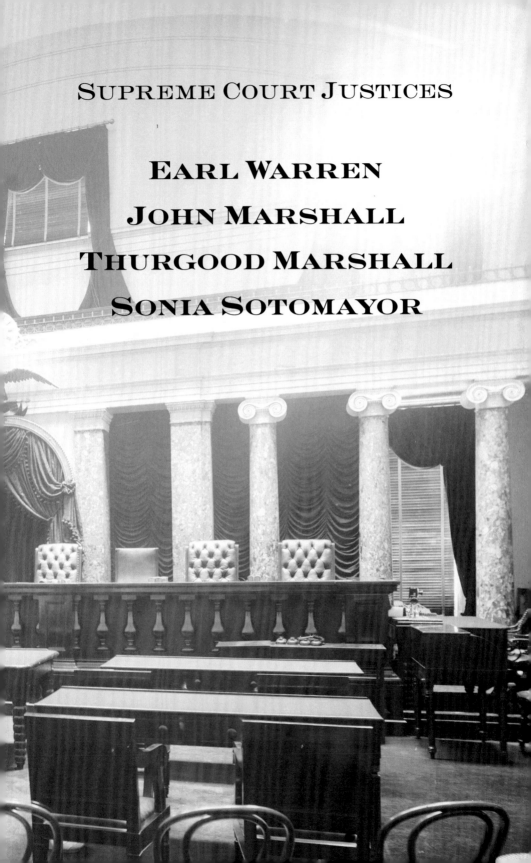

# Supreme Court Justices

## Earl Warren
## John Marshall
## Thurgood Marshall
## Sonia Sotomayor

# Supreme Court Justices: John Marshall

Copyright © 2011 by Morgan Reynolds Publishing

Library of Congress Cataloging-in-Publication Data

Corrigan, Jim.
 Supreme Court justices : the story of John Marshall / by Jim Corrigan.
     p. cm.
 Includes bibliographical references and index.
 ISBN 978-1-59935-159-9
 1. Marshall, John, 1755-1835--Juvenile literature. 2.
Judges--Biography--Juvenile literature. 3.  United States. Supreme
Court.--Biography--Juvenile literature.  I. Title.
 KF8745.M3C637 2011
 347.73'2634--dc22
 [B]
                              2010018801

Printed in the United States of America
First Edition

# CONTENTS

John Marshall

# DEFENDER OF THE CONSTITUTION

**I**n early 1807, America was abuzz with scandal. The young nation watched intently as a startling legal case unfolded. Former Vice President Aaron Burr had been arrested and charged with treason against the United States. John Marshall, the country's most revered judge and chief justice of the U.S. Supreme Court, would be presiding over the case.

The Burr trial presented John Marshall with many challenges. Naturally, it would place him in the national spotlight, but he was unafraid of that. As chief justice, he had handled many high-profile cases. Much more troubling to Marshall were the bitter emotions that this particular case evoked from people.

Aaron Burr was not a popular man. During his time in political office, he proved to be devious and untrustworthy. He was constantly in debt. Three years earlier, Burr killed political rival Alexander Hamilton—one of the nation's founding fathers—in a duel. Now, he was accused of committing the crime of treason. President Thomas Jefferson had already publicly denounced Burr as a traitor, and most Americans strongly agreed. John Marshall was determined to make sure that Burr received a fair trial regardless of the public outcry.

Marshall was also concerned about the dangerous precedent the trial might set. The U.S. Constitution was still a new and largely untested set of laws in 1807, but it did contain a very clear definition of treason. The Constitution stated that in order to be convicted of treason, a person must have either made war against the United States, or provided aid and comfort to its enemies. Marshall saw no direct evidence that Aaron Burr had committed either of these acts. Yet the U.S. government, acting on specific orders from President Jefferson, was trying to convict Burr of treason. John Marshall feared that if Jefferson succeeded, future presidents might abuse their power by threatening treason charges against their political opponents.

As the nation looked on, Burr's trial got underway in Richmond, Virginia, in August 1807. Although he was chief justice, John Marshall presided over the federal court in Richmond when the Supreme Court was not in session. The courtroom was much too small for the enormous crowd of onlookers, so it was moved to the chamber of Virginia's legislature. The task of striking an impartial jury was slow and tedious. Most potential jurors already knew of Burr's alleged misdeeds and held strong opinions about him. At last, a panel of twelve unbiased individuals was chosen and the prosecution began.

The government's lawyers carefully built their case against Aaron Burr. They accused him of assembling a small army of men and sailing

An old European map of North America circa 1843

down the Mississippi River with the intention of attacking New Orleans. They said that Burr planned to carve a separate nation out of America's southwestern territory and install himself as its leader. They also claimed that Burr plotted to attack the Spanish colony of Mexico and add its territory to his newly created empire.

Burr vehemently denied the claims against him. He acknowledged that he had organized a group of sixty followers, and that they had sailed down the Mississippi. But Burr said

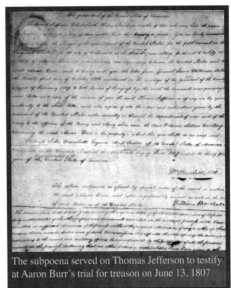

The subpoena served on Thomas Jefferson to testify at Aaron Burr's trial for treason on June 13, 1807

their goal was to find fertile lands on which to establish a farming community. They were settlers, he said, not invaders. The government lawyers persisted, bringing more than a dozen witnesses before the court. The lawyers were attempting to prove that Burr had openly made war against the United States, but no witness could say that he had. The prosecution was only able to establish that Aaron Burr might have considered treasonous acts, not that he actually carried them out.

Before sending the jury off to deliberate, Marshall explained the law regarding treason. The Constitution required proof of an overt act of war against the United States, as seen by two witnesses. Marshall reminded the jurors that none of the testimony they heard had alluded to an overt act of war by Burr. Accordingly, that testimony could not be the basis for convicting him of treason. "The jury have now heard the opinion of the court on the law of the case," Marshall concluded. "They will apply that law to the facts, and will find a verdict of guilty or not guilty as their own consciences may direct."

With no evidence to prove an open act of treason, the jury quickly found Burr not guilty. They then considered the lesser charge of inciting war against Spain, and again arrived at a verdict of not guilty. The trial was over, and Aaron Burr was a free man. President Jefferson was outraged, and so were most of the American people. Much of the furor was directed at John Marshall. Newspapers chastised him for interfering with the trial's outcome. In Baltimore, an angry mob burned his likeness in effigy. Marshall did not care. He had defended the spirit and wording of the Constitution, despite overwhelming pressure to ignore it. In short, he had done his job.

For John Marshall, the Constitution always mattered most. It was the supreme set of laws that held the states together as a unified nation. It also ensured justice for the nation's citizens. From an early age, Marshall understood the importance of liberty, unity, and justice. As a teen, he had witnessed the inequities of colonial rule under Britain. He then joined the Continental Army and fought in the struggle for American independence from Britain. The hard times Marshall experienced as a soldier gave him an undying love for his newly formed country.

After the Revolutionary War, Marshall observed the disorderly and sometimes selfish manner in which the former British colonies—now states—interacted with each other. He came from Virginia, and most of his neighbors thought of themselves as Virginians first, and then only secondly as Americans. The same attitude prevailed in the other twelve states. Each pursued its own interests separately of the rest.

As a young lawyer and politician, Marshall supported the creation of a strong national government. It would provide the states with unity and coordinate their efforts. Before that could happen, though, the states would need to accept—or ratify—the Constitution. Nobody was sure if fiercely independent Virginia would ratify. John Marshall helped convince his fellow Virginians that the Constitution was a good idea, clearing the way for ratification.

Before long, Marshall was serving in the new federal government that he had so vigorously supported. He went to France on a diplomatic mission, and represented America admirably at a time when the two nations were veering toward war. Upon returning home, he was elected to Congress. In 1800, President John Adams chose Marshall as his secretary of state. The following year, Adams appointed him chief justice of the Supreme Court. It was here that John Marshall would make his greatest contributions to the country he loved so dearly.

At the time, the Supreme Court did not enjoy the respect and stature that it does today. The Court had been created by the Constitution, but its role in the government was not yet fully defined. Some people, including Thomas Jefferson, resented the Supreme Court. Jefferson felt it was unnecessary and potentially unsafe, as the Court could possibly interfere with the important work of the president and Congress. For that reason, Jefferson wanted to keep the Court's powers narrow and restricted.

John Marshall felt otherwise. He believed firmly in the system of checks and balances set forth in the Constitution. Under that system, Congress created laws, the president carried them out, and the judiciary had the job of interpreting those laws when a dispute arose. Since the Constitution was a set of

John Marshall

laws, the Supreme Court would handle any questions that arose. And if Congress passed a law or the president gave an executive order that went against the Constitution, the Supreme Court could cancel that law or order.

For the next three and a half decades, John Marshall would build the Court's character and reputation. By the time he finished, the idea of an independent and powerful judiciary was widely accepted. In fact, most people had come to view it as essential. With a series of key decisions in landmark cases, using the Constitution as its guide, the Court mapped out a blueprint of the powers and limitations of government. Marshall and his colleagues weighed the rights of individual citizens and states against the best interests of the nation. Each decision drew varying amounts of praise and criticism, but it was always accepted as final. The supremacy of the Court had been established.

Those who knew John Marshall personally described him as something of an enigma. He was the country's highest-ranking judge, yet he hardly looked the part. Tall and lean, he paid little attention to his clothes or his appearance. He was quiet, leading some to mistakenly assume that he had little to say. Despite his high office, Marshall did not hesitate to perform common work. Richmond neighbors often saw him helping with housecleaning or shopping for groceries at the local market, activities unheard of for a nineteenth-century American gentleman.

Marshall's eyes offered the first clue of his true character. Black and penetrating, they revealed a mind of extraordinary depth and good humor. Even those who disagreed with his legal opinions could not argue with his flawless logic. Scholars marveled over the eloquence of his writings. Most importantly, Marshall was seen universally as fair and honest. No one ever doubted his sincerity or integrity.

Despite his quiet demeanor, John Marshall rarely missed an opportunity to socialize. The chief justice enjoyed good food and fine wine. He routinely hosted elegant dinners and parties in his Richmond home, and was a lifelong member of the city's foremost social club. He easily separated work from play, and showed political adversaries that he was eager to be their friend.

As a young law student, Marshall had learned that heated arguments were best left in the courtroom. Attorneys who clashed while representing their clients could still be friends after the gavel had sounded. Marshall observed this same phenomenon upon reaching elected office. Politicians hurled vicious insults at one another while in session, and then enjoyed a drink together at the local tavern afterward. In this tradition, John Marshall always evaluated a man's character separately from his politics.

His intellect, affability, and evenhandedness made Marshall a natural leader. From the battlefield to the courtroom, men gladly followed him. Soldier, lawyer, politician, and judge were just some of the roles he filled during his lifetime. Marshall was also a savvy real estate investor, building a fortune for his family through insightful land purchases on the American frontier. He was a respected author, using his gift with words to pen a five-volume biography of his hero and late friend, George Washington.

At age fifty-seven, he became an explorer, leading a survey team through harsh Virginia wilderness to plan new roads and canals. The six-week trek was made at the request of the state legislature. Stomping through the thickly wooded mountains must have felt reassuringly familiar to the chief justice. It was in the hostile Virginia backcountry, in the year 1755, that John Marshall's story began.

# Distant Relatives, Bitter Enemies

John Marshall had many political opponents during his lifetime, but very few personal enemies. Yet there was one notable rival who Marshall simply could not abide—Thomas Jefferson. The author of the Declaration of Independence was a dozen years older, and of course a patriot of the highest order, but Marshall considered him snobbish and untrustworthy.

Jefferson, meanwhile, saw Marshall as a devious manipulator, someone who could twist a person's words to mean anything he wanted. Jefferson once said of Marshall, "So great is his sophistry you must never give him an affirmative answer or you will be forced to grant his conclusion. Why, if he were to ask me if it were daylight or not, I'd reply, 'Sir, I don't know, I can't tell.'"

Historians have long debated the source of the friction between Marshall and Jefferson. Their sharply contrasting political viewpoints certainly did not help, but the root of their ill will may have been more personal. Both men traced their ancestry back to the Randolphs, one of Virginia's oldest and most distinguished families. Accordingly, John Marshall and Thomas Jefferson were distant relatives. However, Marshall belonged to an estranged branch of the family tree. His grandmother became an outcast when she eloped with a man of lesser social standing, creating a rift that never closed. The remnants of those strained family ties may have influenced Marshall and Jefferson.

Regardless of its cause, the hostility between these two great Americans worsened as their paths crossed professionally. Both men reached the pinnacle of their careers at almost exactly the same time. Marshall became chief justice in January 1801, and Jefferson was sworn in as America's third president the following March. In the months and years afterward, they would collide over issues of profound importance to the nation.

## LESSONS IN LIFE AND LAW

**N**orth America was still mostly rugged and unspoiled terrain in the mid-eighteenth century. Europeans had begun arriving on the continent's east coast many years earlier. As their numbers grew, the white settlers gradually moved westward, taming the wilderness and displacing the Native American tribes they encountered. It was an era of exploration, conflict, and constant danger. Humans risked death from wild animals, disease, starvation, the elements, and their adversaries. This was the world into which John Marshall was born on September 24, 1755.

His father, Thomas Marshall, was a land surveyor for an English lord who held title to a large swath of northern Virginia. Thomas Marshall had married Mary Randolph Keith a year earlier, and together they established a modest home in the outpost of Germantown. John was their first offspring, but he would not be an only child for long. Large families were typical, and John was joined by fourteen siblings: eight sisters and six brothers. Their parents stressed the importance of education, even for girls, which was not customary at the time. There were no schoolhouses in the area, so

each child in the crowded household learned to read and write from an adult or older sibling.

Young John Marshall developed a passion for reading, but books were scarce on the frontier. To his delight, the English lord who employed his father owned an extensive library and loaned out books freely. John particularly enjoyed poetry and works of history. He spent many hours writing out copies of the passages that captured his imagination. In later life, Marshall would credit this childhood exercise for his prowess as a writer.

The powerful nations of Europe jockeyed to claim their portion of the New World. Britain had successfully established thirteen colonies, including Virginia, but France was making inroads to the north and west. The rivalry led to a military showdown that played itself out while John Marshall was still a boy. France and Britain both formed alliances with various Native American tribes, and then fought for ultimate control of North America. Known as the French and Indian War, it ended in 1763 and was an undeniable British victory. The thirteen colonies were secure.

Although the colonists were safe, they were not happy. The fighting had ended, but thousands of British soldiers stayed, giving colonial cities the feel of a military occupation. Britain's parliament, sensing the colonies were becoming too brash and independent, exerted more control.

The Siege of Fort William Henry in 1757 during the French and Indian War

Parliament made laws demonstrating its power over the colonies, a move Americans deeply resented.

The biggest source of tension was money. Britain had spent enormous sums defending the colonies and was now facing a financial crisis. Colonial merchants, meanwhile, had profited during the French and Indian War by trading goods with other nations—including secret and illegal deals with France. Britain felt it was time for the prosperous colonies to start helping with the financial burden. Parliament began collecting taxes on the goods that Americans liked to trade, such as tea, sugar, and molasses. The tax money would be sent back to Britain to help pay for the costs of the war. Colonists despised the idea of financing a government that dictated to them from the other side of the ocean. They complained that the taxes had been imposed by a parliament they did not help to elect. "No taxation without representation!" became their rally cry.

Tensions boiled over in December 1773, when angry colonists dumped shiploads of tea into Boston Harbor in protest. Following the Boston Tea Party, relations between Britain and the colonies deteriorated rapidly. Parliament tried to clamp down further on the American resistance with more troops and stricter laws. It only made matters worse. Mobs of irate colonists took to the streets, hurling insults and stones at British soldiers. Bloodshed followed, leading to a state of open rebellion in the colonies. The American Revolution was underway.

John Marshall was twenty years old when the colonies formally declared their independence in July 1776. As a teen, he had watched the dispute with Britain escalate, and concluded that a war was likely. Marshall decided to learn the ways of a soldier. In 1775, he

A stamp illustrating the Boston Tea Party. American colonists, dressed as Native Americans, boarded trade ships and threw chests of tea into the harbor, rebelling against Britain's tea tax on American trade.

George Washington at Valley Forge during the American Revolution

joined the local militia, a small collection of farmers and craftsmen who had sworn to protect Virginia. These part-time soldiers, and thousands of others just like them, would go on to form George Washington's Continental Army to fight for independence. As a young scholar and gentleman, John Marshall was a natural choice for the militia's second in command. Lieutenant Marshall taught his fifty or sixty inexperienced troops to march in unison and deploy for battle. They followed his commands with pride and vigor.

The volunteers of Washington's army may have had plenty of enthusiasm, but they lacked virtually everything else. Food, ammunition, and even clothing were always in short supply. The thirteen colonies claimed to be eager for independence, but seemed unwilling to pay for it. A fighting army needs a steady supply of money and fresh troops in order to survive. The colonial governments were reluctant to furnish either. George Washington struggled to hold his destitute army together as he pleaded with Continental Congress for supplies.

The British army, meanwhile, was a formidable enemy. Its legions of soldiers had the best weapons, training, and equipment available. They could rely on support from the British navy, which at the time was the strongest in the world. John Marshall was well aware of the firepower of the British fleet. He had witnessed its bombardment of

Norfolk, Virginia, on New Year's Day, 1776. The destroyed city burned for days. Although a junior officer, Marshall understood the extreme difficulties of defeating the British. He was frustrated with the colonies, especially his native Virginia, for not providing enough resources to give the Continental Army a fighting chance. Each colony seemed satisfied to let the others pull the load.

The war took Marshall and his fellow Virginians northward into places they had never seen, such as Pennsylvania, New York, and New Jersey. Once there, Marshall's superior officers selected him for an elite unit with a special mission. The handpicked group of six hundred infantrymen would harass the British army whenever possible. Their job was to strike without warning, create confusion within the British ranks, and then disappear to plan their next raid. George Washington hoped this tactic would slow the British army and frustrate its leaders. Marshall and his comrades enjoyed some success, but not enough to turn the tide of battle. The Continental Army suffered many defeats. Many of the volunteers lost their fighting spirit, and some deserted the army to return home and look after their families.

For those who remained, the low point came at a barren stretch of land known as Valley Forge, Pennsylvania. The British army had captured Philadelphia, and then settled in for the winter of 1777-1778. George Washington needed to keep his army camped nearby, and he chose the fields of Valley Forge. British troops spent the harsh winter months in warm Philadelphia houses. The Continental troops huddled together in damp log huts. They had no blankets and little food. Their hole-ridden shoes—worn out from the previous year's marching and fighting—offered no protection from frostbite. Diseases such as typhoid and dysentery spread through the camp. At least half of the 12,000 beleaguered troops were unfit for duty. About 3,000 starved, froze to death, or succumbed to illness. Washington worried that by spring he would no longer have an army left to face the British. The War of Independence would be lost.

John Marshall endured the misery of Valley Forge with cheerful optimism, setting an important example for his men. He joked with them about the horrid conditions and told amusing stories to distract them from their suffering. An observer wrote of Marshall, "He was an excellent companion, and idolized by the soldiers and his brother officers, whose gloomy hours were enlivened by his inexhaustible fund of anecdote." A natural athlete, Marshall also challenged the men to foot races. The competition lifted their spirits and kept them in fighting trim.

To Washington's surprise and delight, the Continental Army emerged from Valley Forge stronger than ever. With the thaw of spring, much needed food and supplies began to arrive. Governments in Europe learned of the Americans' plucky determination and decided to send help. Britain's arch-rival, France, dispatched a shipment of 30,000 muskets.

An outstanding French officer named Lafayette was already with the Americans, offering George Washington valuable tactical advice. A German general, von Steuben, came to Valley Forge to train the

A painting circa 1819 depicting the presentation of the Declaration of Independence to Congress

Continental troops. Soon, France would declare war on Britain and enter the conflict as an American ally. British generals sensed the tide of war turning against them. They abandoned Philadelphia and headed toward New York. Many battles remained, but more often the result would be an American victory.

By the end of 1779, John Marshall had risen to the rank of captain. He had fought in the war for more than three years, and the army granted him a leave of absence. Marshall returned home to Virginia to visit his family. His father commanded an artillery regiment in the port of Yorktown, and Marshall went to see him. The trip to Yorktown would be a pivotal moment in John Marshall's life. It was there, in the spring of 1780, that Marshall became acquainted with the two great loves of his life: the woman he would someday marry, and the law.

The single young ladies of Yorktown looked forward to Marshall's arrival. They had heard tales of his battlefield exploits, and considered him a prized bachelor. The ladies imagined a charming and strikingly handsome man, resplendent in his captain's uniform. When John Marshall finally did arrive in Yorktown, they were disappointed. Although tall and friendly, he was not the dashing adventurer they had imagined. The twenty-four-old officer was decidedly plain, and obviously made no attempt to improve his appearance. A frayed uniform hung loosely on his lanky frame, its buttons dull and tarnished. Marshall was quiet and reserved, leading the women to conclude that he had nothing worthwhile to say. They promptly lost interest in him and began looking elsewhere for a potential husband.

Marshall did not go completely ignored, however. He had caught the eye of a young girl named Mary Willis "Polly" Ambler. Polly was shy and just fourteen years of age. She had learned of Marshall from her older sister, who found him highly unsatisfactory, and Polly decided she wanted to meet him. They danced together at a spring cotillion, and

A painting of William and Mary College in Williamsburg, Virginia, in the 1700s

found they had much in common despite the age difference. Polly's family liked Marshall, and he became a regular visitor to their home. He shared with the Amblers his love of books, entertaining them for hours by reading his favorites aloud.

The war was winding down, with American independence seeming virtually guaranteed. Marshall received notice from the army that he did not need to return. The release from service left Marshall with a dilemma—he now had to choose a profession. He could have easily followed his father's example and become a land surveyor on the Virginia frontier. He could also have drawn on his backwoods experience to become a successful farmer. Marshall's friends and family felt he should instead make use of his remarkable gift with words. At their urging, he enrolled in law classes at the College of William and Mary in nearby Williamsburg.

At William and Mary, Marshall had the good fortune to study under the esteemed judge and law professor George Wythe. A signer of the Declaration of Independence, Wythe made many valuable contributions to the American legal system. Among these was his innovative work at William and Mary, where he educated some of the new nation's sharpest young minds. His foremost students included not only Marshall, but also Thomas Jefferson, James Monroe, and Henry Clay. Wythe's lectures organized a murky and rapidly evolving body of common law into understandable themes. To reinforce his classroom lessons, Wythe held moot court and mock legislatures. These practice sessions enabled his students to develop their powers of reason through fictional trials and debates. Marshall kept a detailed notebook of Wythe's teachings, and referred to it often throughout his long career.

Marshall completed his studies and passed Virginia's bar exam, but soon found there was no work available for a new lawyer. The war had not yet officially ended, and the courts remained closed. With no cases being heard, Marshall could not earn a living by representing clients. He needed a different job until the courts reopened, and that of politician seemed to match his skills. After all, politicians created the laws in which attorneys toiled. In 1782, Marshall ran for a seat in the Virginia House of Delegates. Voters found him to be straightforward and trustworthy, so they elected him to office. At age twenty-six, Marshall journeyed to Richmond for his first term of public service. The part-time job paid only a modest salary and travel stipend, but it was a start.

Like the voters, Marshall's fellow delegates instinctively liked him. After just six months in office, they selected him to fill a vacancy on Virginia's council of state. The council of state was an eight-person team that advised the governor. Membership on the council was a prestigious post. A full-time job, it paid much better than the legislature, and it gave Marshall the opportunity to directly influence the course of Virginia's affairs. He was grateful for the appointment, which turned out not to be based solely on merit. Polly's father, a wealthy and influential man named Jaquelin Ambler, lobbied his friends in the legislature for it. Marshall had been courting Polly for some time, and a marriage seemed likely. By securing Marshall's appointment to the council of state, Jaquelin Ambler was assisting his future son-in-law. As expected, Marshall and Polly became engaged and married in early 1783.

John Marshall was enjoying his run of good fortune, but something troubled him—he longed for the work in which he was trained. The war had finally ended, and the courts were reopened. Marshall would have to choose between the financial security of his government position, and the thrill of arguing cases before a judge and jury. He was a lawyer at heart, and knew that he ultimately belonged in a courtroom.

# FRIENDSHIP WITH
# GEORGE WASHINGTON

Service in the Continental Army made many strong impressions on John Marshall. For the rest of his life, he would treasure the brotherhood he felt with his fellow soldiers as they faced danger and hardship together. The war also strengthened his belief in America as a unified nation, not just a collection of independent states. Finally, Marshall developed an everlasting respect and admiration for the army's leader, George Washington. In later years, the two men would become good friends.

Washington was nearly a quarter-century older, but he and Marshall shared a common background. They were both Virginians who knew farming and frontier life. As young men, they were both anxious to acquire wealth, but later realized that greater rewards existed than money. They shared a love for their nation, and were destined to spend most of their lives in its service. It is likely that Washington saw much of himself in his younger friend. The first president was eager to have Marshall as part of his cabinet, but Marshall respectfully declined. At that point in his life, Marshall was still preoccupied with money, and federal jobs paid little.

John Marshall almost certainly viewed Washington as a role model and mentor. Whenever Washington's name came up in letters and conversation, Marshall always spoke glowingly of his friend. On more than one occasion, he traveled to Mount Vernon to seek the elder man's advice. When the former first president died in 1799, Marshall solemnly delivered his eulogy before Congress, and then led a funeral procession through the nation's capital. Afterward, Marshall embarked on a meticulous biography of Washington that is still in print today. It was a final tribute to his hero and beloved friend.

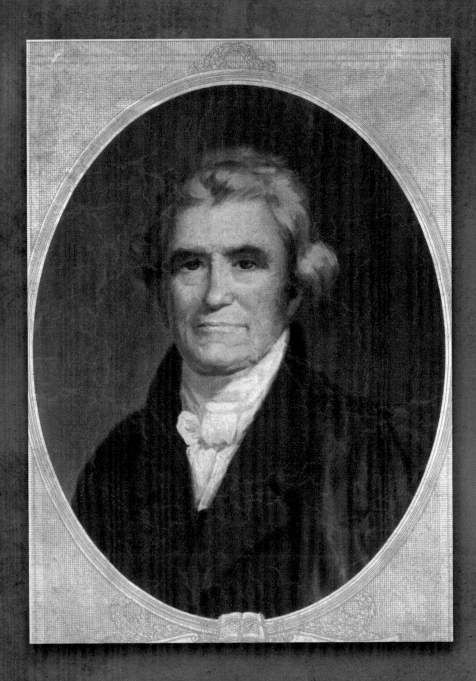

John Marshall

# LAWYER AND LEADER

By 1784, the name John Marshall was well known throughout Richmond and elsewhere in Virginia. Although not yet thirty, Marshall had become a respected figure in state politics. His colleagues on the council of state valued his deep knowledge of the law, and the governor frequently sought his legal counsel. Marshall maintained a modest Richmond law practice during his time in state government. As word spread of his abilities, the practice's client list began to grow. Marshall could no longer split his time between the two jobs. He would need to pick one over the other.

Marshall chose his law practice. He resigned from the council of state and dedicated himself to his clients. As a compromise, he once again ran for a seat in the House of Delegates and won. The legislature required only a small amount of his time, yet kept him closely involved with Virginia politics. Marshall was also thrilled to devote some of his time to a new role—that of father. Polly gave birth to their first child, a son named Thomas, in July 1784. A daughter named Rebecca followed, but tragically she lived for only five days.

Marshall gradually overcame his grief, but Polly did not. She suffered a mental collapse and never fully recovered.

National events garnered Marshall's attention in 1786. A mob of Massachusetts farmers led by former soldier Daniel Shays were threatening rebellion. Angered by high land taxes, the farmers stormed state government buildings and threatened revolt. Local militia eventually quelled Shays' Rebellion, but it was not an isolated incident. People across the country were dissatisfied with what they perceived as

The first page of the Constitution of the United States

unfair laws and ineffective leaders. Uprisings were becoming common, and state governments seemed unable to cope.

John Marshall agreed with a growing sentiment that America needed a stronger national government. This federal government would unify the states and establish a fair set of laws that applied uniformly across the entire nation. In 1787, a group of fifty-five delegates from across the states gathered in Philadelphia, which at the time was the nation's capital. The delegates labored for four long months to create a blueprint of the new federal government—the Constitution.

The Constitution described the new government's form and function. There would be three main pieces or branches: Congress, the president, and the courts. Each branch would hold some authority over the other two, ensuring that none became too powerful. Similarly, the thirteen states of the Union would remain independent, but they would be obligated to obey all federal laws. For John Marshall and those who shared his outlook, the proposed Constitution was the perfect remedy to America's problems. Other people looked on it with skepticism and disdain. They envisioned an all-powerful government headed by a president who acted more like a tyrant. As they saw it, the Constitution stripped states of their right to self-govern.

Each of the thirteen states had to ratify the Constitution before it could go into effect. The outcome was doubtful. Quarrels over ratification came to dominate living rooms, town halls, and the legislatures of every state. In Virginia, trouble started almost as soon as the House of Delegates began examining the Constitution. Legislators favoring it clashed sharply with those who opposed it. From his House seat, Marshall looked on with alarm. He feared the bickering might prevent any thoughtful debate on the Constitution. The feuding legislators might yield to their emotions, either supporting or opposing ratification without first giving it reflective thought.

To avoid a showdown between the two factions, Marshall stood up and calmly asked to speak. In a thoughtful voice, he noted that a matter of such grave importance should not be decided hastily. He also suggested that it might be wise to involve the citizens of Virginia in the decision-making process. Marshall therefore proposed that the Constitution "be submitted to a convention of the people, for their full and free investigation and discussion." The other legislators considered

Patrick Henry

Marshall's motion reasonable. Virginia would hold a special convention of citizens to debate ratification of the Constitution.

As a respected leader in his community, Marshall was among those chosen to participate in the convention. Many other esteemed Virginians would be present as well, including future presidents James Madison and James Monroe. But the undeniable celebrity of the convention was Patrick Henry. An eloquent attorney and firebrand of the Revolution, it was Henry who had once uttered those famous words, "Give me liberty or give me death!" Patrick Henry commanded the respect and admiration of everyone in attendance at the convention, including Marshall. Yet he posed a unique problem for those who favored ratification. Henry ardently supported the rights of states and individuals, and he viewed a strong federal government as a threat to those rights. His status and viewpoint made Patrick Henry the natural leader of the anti-federalists, the name given to those who opposed the ratification of the Constitution. When the special convention assembled in June 1788, John Marshall was only thirty-two years old. He did not yet have the wisdom and experience to lead the federalist cause. Some of the more senior delegates would

fill that role. Marshall would naturally support their arguments during the convention's long, drawn-out debates. But he knew he could help in another way as well. As scores of delegates converged on Richmond from all across Virginia, Marshall decided to play host.

The Marshall home sat just a few short blocks from the convention meeting place. After a long day of deliberations, the tired attendees would undoubtedly welcome a fine meal with good company.

James Madison, fourth president of the United States

Marshall genuinely enjoyed throwing parties, but in this instance he had another motive. An astute politician, he understood the value of geniality in shaping opinion. The lavish dinners would give him a subtle opportunity to influence the convention's outcome. As his guests dined, he could promote the many benefits of the Constitution, perhaps persuading some skeptics to vote in favor of ratification. To carry out his plan, Marshall purchased large quantities of the best food and wine available.

As expected, the convention promptly turned into a verbal duel between Virginia's elder statesmen. Patrick Henry spoke flawlessly on behalf of the anti-federalists, describing their vision of an America run by a smothering national government and its despotic president. James Madison led the federalists. Madison had been present at the Philadelphia Convention a year earlier, and had been a primary architect of the Constitution. While Patrick Henry's speeches blazed with emotion, Madison's were calm and rational. With cool precision, he addressed each of Henry's assertions, and explained the intent behind each article of the Constitution.

During the debates, John Marshall rose to speak only occasionally, and then spoke sparingly. Most of his comments addressed details of the proposed federal court system. His keen observations about the judiciary quickly earned him a reputation as an expert on the matter. Meanwhile, Marshall's after-hours dinner parties became enormously popular. Federalist friends and foes alike attended the meals, and the good will and hospitality they shared during Marshall's gatherings helped keep convention debates civil.

Ultimately, James Madison's watertight logic extinguished the impassioned pleas of Patrick Henry. The convention swayed slightly from a deadlock toward favoring the Constitution. By a tally of eighty-nine to seventy-nine, the delegates narrowly approved Virginia's ratification. Although defeated, Patrick Henry and his followers made a profound contribution to the process. Based on their concerns, the convention proposed a series of amendments to the Constitution. These amendments sought to restrain the new national government from trampling Americans' freedom of speech and other personal liberties. The Virginia proposal went on to form the foundation of the Constitution's Bill of Rights. John Marshall heartily approved.

Marshall was pleased with his role in securing Virginia's ratification.

Patrick Henry denounces the imposition of the Stamp Act on the American colonists in 1765.

He viewed it as the crowning achievement of his political career. Considering his work now finished, he resigned from the state legislature. He planned to devote himself fully to the business of being a lawyer.

George Washington had other ideas. In 1789, the first president appointed his friend the United States attorney for Virginia. (U.S. attorneys represent the federal government in court.) Congress confirmed the appointment, but Marshall respectfully declined. He thanked Washington for the high honor, but explained that the demands of his law practice left no time for government service. Washington was no doubt aware that a private practice lawyer earned far more than the meager salary then paid to a U.S. attorney. He may have hoped that Marshall would be compelled by a factor other than money. Marshall, however, had to worry about supporting a growing family. His wife Polly would ultimately give birth to ten children.

The next few years of John Marshall's life followed the path he had envisioned when first studying law at the College of William and Mary. He was a busy attorney, stepping frequently into the courtroom to argue on behalf of his clients. Most of the cases he handled were financial in nature, such as a dispute over a debt or conflicting claims to the same tract of land. But there were exceptions, and in 1792, Marshall made a rare foray into criminal law. The case came to be known as the Bizarre murder inquest. Bizarre was the name of the accused man's plantation, but the word also accurately described this sordid legal case.

Richard Randolph, the wealthy owner of the Bizarre plantation, was

George Washington, first president of the United States

rumored to have had an affair with his wife's sister, Nancy. As the story went, the relationship produced an illegitimate child, which Richard Randolph was said to have murdered. Virginia's social scene hummed for months with gossip about this tawdry episode. Randolph had yet to be charged with a crime, since no corpse had been found and there were no witnesses to the alleged murder. Yet the rumors and gossip persisted, and most people came to accept them as true. Unwilling to go through life as an outcast, Randolph sought out Marshall's legal counsel.

Marshall reviewed the case and recognized a clear lack of evidence and facts. He advised Randolph to go before the local magistrate and request an inquiry to clear his name. Marshall expected the matter to be promptly dismissed. To his surprise, the court took Randolph into custody and launched an official inquest, summoning seventeen witnesses to testify about what they knew.

The witnesses told the court that a year earlier Nancy was engaged to be married, but her fiancée had suddenly become ill and died. In the weeks afterward, Randolph was frequently seen consoling his sister-in-law, sometimes holding her in a tender embrace. Other witnesses soon noticed a change in Nancy's appearance that led them to conclude she was pregnant. On the night of October 1, 1792, Richard Randolph, his wife Judith, and Nancy were staying at the estate of family friends. Nancy excused herself from dinner, saying that she was unwell. Soon after, Richard and Judith retired to an adjoining bedroom.

Late that night, a woman's screams echoed through the upstairs hallway. The lady of the estate went to Nancy's bedroom but found the door locked. When she knocked, Richard answered and assured her that Nancy was resting comfortably. After her guests departed, the lady examined Nancy's bed and found bloodstains. A servant advised her that Nancy had suffered a miscarriage. Weeks later, the manor's slaves reported that they had discovered a fetus on a garden woodpile, and discreetly disposed of it.

This testimony may not have reflected well on his client, but Marshall knew that it offered no proof of a crime. He brought in Patrick Henry—the master orator and champion of states rights—to cross-examine the witnesses. Although Marshall and Henry had their political differences, they admired each other personally and professionally. They enjoyed working together and made a powerful courtroom tandem. Marshall designed the legal strategy, and Patrick Henry put it into action. Before the Bizarre inquest was over, Henry had not only convinced the panel of magistrates that Randolph was innocent, but most of the witnesses and spectators as well. When the magistrates announced their not-guilty verdict, the courtroom gallery erupted in cheers.

Richard Randolph was vindicated, but he never recovered from the emotional distress. He withdrew from society and died just three years later. Nancy left Virginia to become a schoolteacher in New York. She remained silent about the true circumstances surrounding the Bizarre incident until many years later, when she confided in Richard's stepfather. Nancy explained that she had indeed become pregnant, but with her fiancée's child. The fiancée died shortly afterward, and Nancy faced the scorn of being an unwed mother in eighteenth-century Virginia. Her child, however, was a stillborn. Nancy said that Richard had helped her through the entire ordeal and then vowed to remain silent in order to protect her honor. She credited him as being a gentleman of the highest order.

It is unclear whether Marshall knew these details as he conducted Richard Randolph's defense. Either way, it would not have mattered. Marshall's duty as an officer of the court was to provide his client with the best legal defense possible, and he did precisely that. The Bizarre episode was not typical of the cases John Marshall handled during his career as a lawyer, but it did highlight his courtroom skills and his ability to collaborate with other great legal minds. Marshall valued cooperation, and in future years he would use teamwork to reach heights that no individual could achieve alone.

# MARSHALL THE SOCIALITE

Although quiet and reserved, John Marshall earnestly enjoyed the company of others. He routinely attended parties, sporting events, and the theater. In 1788, Marshall became a founding member of Richmond's first social club for men. Members of the Quoits Club, also known as the Barbecue Club, met every Saturday during the summer months.

Quoits was a pitch-and-toss game played with brass rings and a metal spike staked into the ground. It resembled the modern game of horseshoes. Quoits was one of Marshall's favorite pastimes, and he was among the club's best players. Club meetings began with a catered lunch of ham, mutton, and of course, barbecue. As they ate, the thirty to forty members enjoyed a special beverage prepared by Marshall himself. It was a powerful fruit punch containing brandy, rum, and wine. Marshall was particularly fond of a fortified Portuguese wine called Madeira, and he sprinkled it liberally into the concoction.

After lunch, the quoits competition got underway. Marshall took the games seriously and frequently got down on his hands and knees to measure the distance between rings and spike. Some of Richmond's most prominent citizens belonged to the club, including doctors, politicians, attorneys, and merchants. Only one rule was strictly enforced—members could not discuss business, religion, or politics during a meeting. Violators of this rule were required to buy the club a case of champagne. Marshall remained a lifelong member, pitching quoits on breezy summer Saturdays until the year of his death. As a tribute to their late friend, the members of Richmond's Quoits Club voted to leave John Marshall's seat vacant forever.

The mountains of Virginia

# MISSION TO FRANCE

**B**y 1795, Marshall was at the pinnacle of his success as an attorney. His law practice thrived, and with his earnings he bought many acres of land in Virginia and Kentucky. At last, he was achieving the financial success he had always wanted, and refused any distractions. George Washington once more tried to coax Marshall into federal service, offering him the position of U.S. attorney general. As before, Marshall thanked the president but respectfully declined, citing the demands of his practice.

A year later, Washington tried again. The nation needed a new minister to France, and nothing would please the president more, he said, than if Marshall accepted the job and went to France to negotiate with that country. Again, Marshall resisted. An enormous land title case, one in which Marshall held a personal stake and had labored at for years, was finally coming to its conclusion. He simply could not afford to abandon it. Washington understood, but did not abandon the idea of eventually enlisting John Marshall into the service of the nation.

The president's latest offer demonstrated his deep confidence in Marshall's abilities. Relations between France and the United States

John Adams, second president of the United States

were deteriorating rapidly, and Washington desperately needed a minister who could restore them. France was a close ally during the American Revolution, but much had changed since then. The French experienced a revolution of their own, one in which they deposed their king and experimented with other forms of government. The French Revolution was a tumultuous and bloody affair in which various factions competed for power. In 1795, a five-man council called the Directory took control. The Directory disliked America's warming relationship with Britain, and took out its anger on U.S. ships at sea. French naval vessels began assaulting American merchant ships and seizing their cargo.

The seizures posed a major problem for John Adams, who succeeded Washington as president in 1797. America's navy was far too small to protect the cargo ships, which were vital to the growing U.S. economy. American diplomats in Paris tried to negotiate a solution, but the Directory seemed uninterested. Meanwhile, the attacks at sea continued, and John Adams feared that the two nations were headed toward war. If that happened, America would be at a serious disadvantage. France wielded far greater military and economic resources. The United States might end up facing a French invasion.

Adams decided to make one more diplomatic attempt. This time he would dispatch a team of three special negotiators. He believed it would demonstrate America's sincere desire to resolve the matter. Further, Adams supposed that a three-member team could combine their skills, perhaps reaching a solution that might otherwise elude a single envoy. For the plan to work, Adams needed to choose his team wisely. His first choice was Charles Cotesworth Pinckney, a skilled diplomat who had just returned from Paris on the most recent failed mission. Second was Elbridge Gerry of Massachusetts, a close and respected friend of the president. To complete his team, Adams called on John Marshall. Although not a seasoned diplomat, Marshall was intimately familiar with the details of the Franco-American dispute. He also grasped the nuances of international relations, and was a persuasive advocate.

Marshall received the president's offer via mail, and this time he immediately accepted. He packed and arranged his travel plans; he was going to France. To some, it may have seemed odd that Marshall so readily accepted the assignment. He had, after all, turned down numerous offers from George Washington for government posts, including minister to France. Now, suddenly, he was agreeing to sail abroad on a desperate mission for a president whom he had never met.

To Marshall, there was a fundamental difference between Washington's job offers and the request from John Adams. The mission to Paris was only temporary. Marshall could take a brief absence from his law practice, returning to it as soon as the trip was over. As he explained, "My clients would know immediately that I should soon return and I could make arrangements with the gentlemen of the bar which would prevent my business from suffering in the meantime." After leaving his cases in the hands of trusted colleagues, John Marshall departed for the first overseas adventure of his life.

He needed to make an important stop first: Mount Vernon, the home of George Washington. By this time, the former president was sixty-five years old and enjoying retirement. Washington understood the French

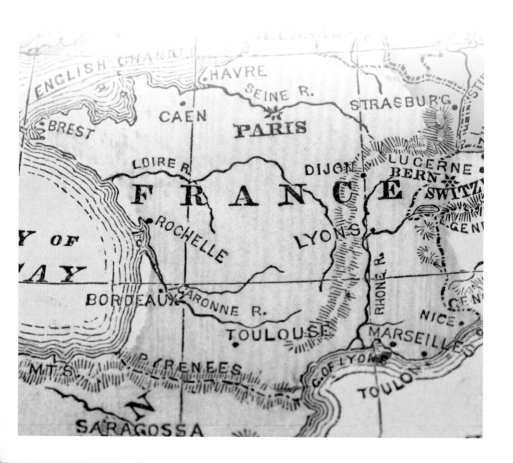

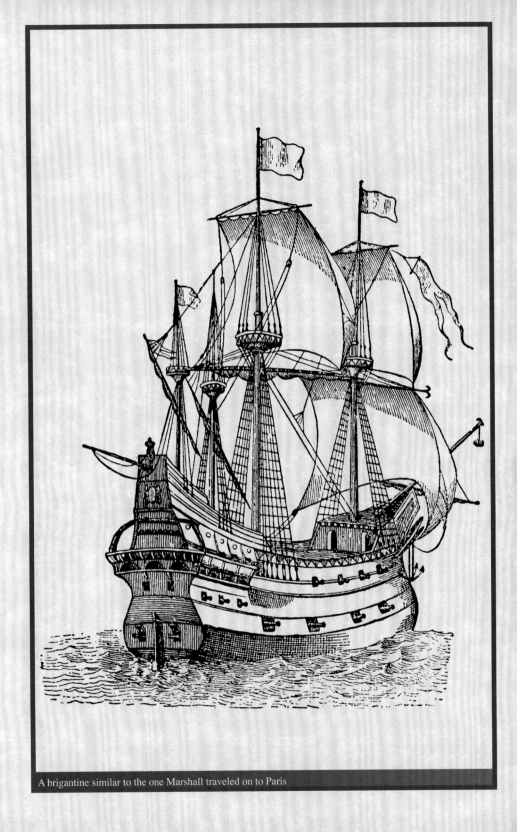

A brigantine similar to the one Marshall traveled on to Paris

French statesman Charles Maurice de Talleyrand

way of thinking, and Marshall wanted the benefit of his advice. The two men spent an entire day conferring, and then Marshall boarded a ship bound for Philadelphia. At the nation's capital, he met with John Adams for some final instructions on how to conduct the mission. Upon assuring the president that he would do his best, Marshall set out across the Atlantic. It was July 1797, and the calm summer winds were making a slow journey for sailing ships. Marshall's brigantine arrived in the Netherlands after a six-week voyage. There he awaited his two colleagues, who had sailed separately.

Another month passed before all three diplomats were together in Paris. Eager to begin the negotiations, they paid a visit to the French foreign minister, a man named Talleyrand. Privately, Talleyrand believed that France should resolve its differences with the United States, but he felt no urgency to do so. He believed he could take his time before convincing his bosses in the Directory to halt the attacks on U.S. shipping. In the meantime, he could toy with the three American envoys, and perhaps coax a bribe for himself in the process. Bribery was an unspoken tradition in French diplomacy, a custom with which the Americans were unfamiliar. Unknown to them, high-ranking French officials like Talleyrand collected far more bribe money each year than they did in salary.

Talleyrand began his ploy by lowering the envoys' expectations of success. He told the Americans that the Directory ministers were very upset with the United States. They strongly disapproved of the Jay Treaty, which normalized relations between America and Britain. The ministers also felt outrage over a speech that President Adams had recently delivered to Congress, in which he insulted French honor. (In reality, Adams's speech made only a passing reference to France.) Talleyrand said that these offenses made the prospect of forging a peaceful agreement highly unlikely. With dramatic flourish, Talleyrand then softened his tone. He promised the American diplomats that he would do his best to help them. Of course, Talleyrand added, his influence might be more effective if he first had a douceur—a monetary gift to sweeten the deal.

The three Americans were baffled as they departed Talleyrand's office. The bribery of government officials seemed to them an underhanded way of doing business. Further, they were insulted both personally and professionally. As official emissaries of the United States, they should not be required to pay for the privilege to negotiate with another nation. Marshall and his colleagues decided to ignore Talleyrand's request. Hopefully, they felt, the Frenchman would drop the matter.

He did not. When the bribe failed to arrive, Talleyrand sent an aide to the U.S. lodgings in Paris. The representative made it clear that a monetary tribute to Talleyrand was required. The Americans declined, stating that they had no authorization from their government to pay a bribe. A diplomatic standoff ensued, with both sides refusing to yield. The situation dragged on for months. Periodically, a Talleyrand representative showed up at the Americans' doorstep, emphasizing the necessity of a bribe. Each time, the reply was no. The French foreign minister attempted to ratchet up the pressure on his guests, hinting that they might soon be expelled from the country.

An engraving of Mount Vernon by John S. C. Abbott in 1866

Although frustrated by the wasted time, the Americans remained firm. John Marshall wrote long reports to the U.S. secretary of state, detailing French attempts to secure a bribe. To rally public support, the secretary of state released Marshall's reports to American newspapers, but first he struck the names of Talleyrand's representatives. In the public version, they were referenced only as agents X, Y, and Z. Americans were outraged by the shabby treatment of their diplomats in what came to be called the XYZ Affair. In France, an embarrassed Talleyrand carried out his threat to expel the diplomats. John Marshall would be coming home.

In June 1798, Marshall returned to the United States a national hero. People lauded the feisty resolve the American negotiators had shown as they withstood the French demands. In Philadelphia, Marshall found himself the guest of honor at a huge parade. He passed through other cities on his way back to Richmond, and received similar greetings. The XYZ Affair had transformed America's spirit. Rather than dreading a war with France, many people now openly called for it.

Marshall arrived home in Richmond with mixed emotions. He had failed in his mission to secure a peace treaty with France, but suddenly that no longer seemed to matter. He and his colleagues had inadvertently become the catalyst for a much-needed surge of patriotism. In the end, that proved a far greater accomplishment. Marshall was also pleased to find his Richmond law practice intact. His fellow attorneys had kept their word and looked after his clients. However, his wife Polly was in frail health. Her depression had worsened during his absence. Polly remained hidden away in her bedroom, secluded from the rest of the world.

A few months later, as Marshall was still settling back into his normal routine, he received an invitation from George Washington to visit Mount Vernon. Washington said he had urgent business to discuss. The former president also invited his nephew, Bushrod Washington, who Marshall knew as a colleague from the Richmond bar. When the two attorneys arrived at Mount Vernon, George Washington wasted no time revealing his purpose.

America was in peril, he explained. A war with France loomed, but there was another and perhaps even greater threat. Washington felt that the country was at risk of tearing itself apart. Although the Constitution had been adopted more than a decade earlier, the fundamental dispute it triggered—that between states rights and a strong federal government—

remained. In the years since ratification, the two groups had organized into formal political parties. The states rights supporters called themselves the Democratic Republicans, and were led by Thomas Jefferson. President John Adams, meanwhile, led the Federalists. The two parties clashed viciously in Congress, creating tensions that stretched across the entire nation.

Although retired from public service, George Washington maintained an active interest in politics. He said he wanted to see the Federalists win control of Congress in the upcoming elections, especially if reasonable men of sound judgment could fill those seats. At that moment, Washington turned to his guests. He said he believed them to be precisely the type of men so desperately needed in Congress. He urged them both to become candidates for the U.S. House of Representatives.

Bushrod Washington expressed reluctance, but after some prodding from his uncle, he eventually agreed. Marshall, however, remained unwilling. He had spent nearly a year overseas in France, and he wanted to return to his law practice. George Washington had heard similar excuses from Marshall in the past, but this time he was adamant. For two days he counseled Marshall, each time underscoring the urgency of his request. It was vital for the health of the nation, Washington said. Marshall continued to respectfully decline.

On the third day of his visit, Marshall decided to rise early and quietly slip out of Mount Vernon. He felt it would be the easiest and most graceful way to leave without disappointing his host further. But as he stepped outside into the cool morning air, Washington was there waiting. The old general had anticipated his adversary's dawn retreat, and now launched his final persuasive assault. Marshall found he could no longer let down the man he so deeply respected and admired. As they stood on the veranda overlooking Washington's estate, Marshall finally acquiesced. He would run for Congress.

John Marshall was no stranger to political campaigns. He had previously been elected to state office on several occasions. While running for Congress in 1799, he employed the same strategy that had worked so well for him in the past. Simply, he used every opportunity to go out among the voters and talk with them about their concerns. He attended parties, barbecues, and public gatherings of every kind.

Of particular concern to voters in 1799 were the Alien and Sedition

Acts. The Federalist Party had recently pushed these acts through Congress, and President John Adams—the Federalist leader—had signed them into law. Among other things, the Alien and Sedition Acts limited people's ability to criticize the U.S. government. Under the laws, anyone who published a criticism of the government, the president, or Congress could be sent to jail for up to five years. Many Americans considered it an unnecessary infringement on the Constitution's guarantee of free speech. Virginia voters wanted to know John Marshall's feelings on the matter.

Marshall told them frankly that, although he was a Federalist, he did not support the Alien and Sedition Acts. He called the acts "useless," and said that "they are calculated to create, unnecessarily, discontents and jealousies at a time when our very existence, as a nation, may depend on our union." The voters valued Marshall's willingness to follow his conscience, even when it meant going against his own political party. When the ballots were tallied on election day, Marshall was the victor. It had been extremely close—a margin of just 114 votes—but he had won a seat in the U.S. House of Representatives.

John Marshall in his plain black justice's robes

# IN SERVICE OF THE NATION

**I**n Congress, the feuding between the Federalists and the Democratic Republicans was worse than ever. Marshall immediately established himself as a voice of moderation. Although a party member, he refused to automatically take the Federalist side.

He examined the issues based on their merit, and voted only for bills that he felt advanced the interests of the nation. In early 1800, the threat of war with France was receding, and the Democratic Republicans proposed cutting back heavily on military spending. Marshall felt the measure was premature, so he opposed it. However, when the same Democratic Republicans later attempted to repeal the hated Sedition Act, Marshall supported them. (Their attempt failed, but the Sedition Act expired in 1801 and was not renewed.) Marshall's free thinking and independence confounded Federalist leaders.

One Federalist leader who actually admired Marshall's autonomy was John Adams. Like Marshall, the president was a moderate. Both men wanted a strong federal government, but they also believed in restraint and compromise. They preferred cooperation over conflict, a trait that many other Federalists viewed as weakness. Increasingly, the Federalist

Party was becoming radical. Its members in Congress were consumed with crushing the Democratic Republicans, and they grew frustrated with their moderate president. John Adams soon found himself being attacked not only by the opposition, but by his own party. During this time, Marshall frequently took the floor to defend the president and his policies.

In May 1800, Adams was searching for a new secretary of state. The last man to hold the job had been ineffective. Today, the U.S. Department of State has roughly 19,000 employees who are responsible

The United States Capitol in Washington, D.C.

for America's foreign relations. In 1800, the State Department handled far more than just diplomacy. Its nine employees also oversaw the daily operations of the federal government. Printing money, issuing copyrights, and taking the census were just some of the tasks supervised by the secretary of state. It was a daunting job, and President Adams chose John Marshall for it. The president felt he could trust Marshall, based on his conduct during the XYZ Affair and in Congress. He also knew Marshall was a man who could get things done.

Marshall did not hesitate to accept the offer. In Congress, he held just one vote among many, so his influence was limited. As secretary of state, he would directly control a large portion of the federal government. His decisions would have an immediate and lasting effect on the nation. When Marshall took the office in June 1800, there was an additional task awaiting him. The federal government was moving from its original home in Philadelphia to the newly established capital of Washington, D.C. Virginia and Maryland had both ceded land for the new city, and an army of workers were hastily constructing enormous government buildings. President Adams wanted no part of the countless details associated with such a massive undertaking. He instructed Marshall to supervise the move, and stressed that the new Capitol building had to be ready for Congress when it reconvened in the fall. Adams then departed for Massachusetts, where he would enjoy a summer vacation. With the president out of town, John Marshall was effectively in charge of the entire federal government.

Marshall threw himself fully into his assigned tasks. The pace of construction quickened further, and the federal bureaucracy packed itself up and moved without incident. When Adams arrived in Washington, D.C., that autumn, not only was the Capitol building ready to receive Congress, the president's mansion was also finished and ready for his family. During the transition, Marshall had seen to America's foreign interests as well. He smoothed over relations with France and Britain, putting the nation on solid diplomatic ground with both powers. As John Adams suspected, he had left the government in highly capable hands.

Adams's time in Washington would be brief. In November 1800, Americans would be once again going to the polls to choose their president. Adams hoped for reelection, but his chances were slim. His party, the Federalists, had become too extreme in their quest for a strong national government. The Alien and Sedition Acts, plus other Federalist attempts to silence their critics, convinced many people that it was time for a change. Voters swept most Federalist candidates from office, including President Adams. They replaced him with Thomas Jefferson, the leader of the Democratic Republicans. John Marshall packed his belongings and prepared to return to Richmond. Clearly, there would be no place for him in Jefferson's administration. Aside from belonging to opposing parties, the two men strongly disliked each other.

John Adams still had a few important duties to perform during his remaining weeks as president. Among them was the need to select a new chief justice of the U.S. Supreme Court. The sitting chief justice had recently announced his resignation. Adams offered the job to John Jay, an American statesman and the governor of New York. Jay had previously served on the Supreme Court as its first chief justice, but he had no interest in returning. Jay politely refused the offer. John Marshall had the duty of informing the president of Jay's decision. He described the unexpected turn of events that followed:

> When I waited on the President with Mr. Jay's letter declining the appointment he said thoughtfully, "Who shall I nominate now?" I replied that I could not tell. . . . After a moment's hesitation he said, "I believe I must nominate you." I had never before heard myself named for the office and had not even thought of it. I was pleased as well as surprised, and bowed in silence. Next day I was nominated.

By choosing Marshall, John Adams was being practical. His time as president was running short, and he could no longer await a reply from a far away candidate, as he had with Jay. Further, although Supreme Court justices are appointed for life, they must first be approved by the Senate. Adams knew that some senators might object to Marshall as being too politically moderate for their own taste, but ultimately they would have no cause to reject him. Finally, the outgoing president could rest assured that he was leaving the Supreme Court in the care of a talented, hard-working man, a man who thought much the same way he did.

Just as Adams anticipated, some senators initially complained about his choice, but in the end they approved it. On January 27, 1801, John Marshall became the fourth chief justice of the United States. He was forty-five years old. His brief periods in Congress and the State Department had enabled him to experience the government's legislative and executive branches. Now he was moving to its judicial branch, the one for which he was best suited. As the Supreme Court convened for its winter term, Marshall prepared to take his place as its leader.

His new job was not nearly as prestigious as it may have sounded. Despite drawing authority directly from the Constitution, the Supreme

Court commanded little influence or even respect. Unlike Congress or the presidency, its purpose was not yet clearly defined. As a result, the Court had languished during its first dozen years of existence. It decided an average of only five cases per year, few of which held any national significance. During this period, nominees to the Court often declined to serve. Some justices who did accept failed to attend on a regular basis, forcing the Court to delay sessions or cancel them entirely. The U.S. Supreme Court was so insignificant that the architects of Washington, D.C., had failed to build it a home. As a result, the nation's highest court held its proceedings wherever it could find space. For a while, it met in a spare office in the Library of Congress. Later, carpenters built it a makeshift courtroom in the Capitol's basement.

John Marshall's goal was to transform the Court into a steadfast judicial institution worthy of the nation's trust and respect. He started with small, symbolic measures. Until this point, Supreme Court justices typically wore flashy, brightly colored robes in the European tradition. The garish garments were intended to reflect power and prestige. When Marshall arrived on his first day to take the oath of chief justice, he wore plain, black robes. With the simple but dignified attire, he was making a powerful statement to the public and to his fellow justices. The Supreme Court was here to work for the people

Chief Justices of the United States. John Marshall is pictured left and center.

of the United States, and it took its duties seriously. Before long, Marshall's colleagues began wearing plain, black robes too.

Marshall wanted the Court to be more than just a collection of judges. He wanted them to be a team. Previously, the justices lived and worked independently, coming together only for formal sessions of the Court. Marshall thought there should be more discussion and interaction among them. They would benefit from the opportunity to exchange ideas and thrash out cases in a more casual setting, he felt. For the next session, Marshall booked rooms for himself and his colleagues at a nearby boardinghouse. By living and dining together, the justices would come to know one another beyond the work environment. They would develop a personal rapport, and gain valuable insight into each other's point of view. In short, they would become a team.

As the highest judicial body in the land, Marshall thought the Supreme Court should speak with a single, unified voice. When deciding a case in the past, each justice issued his own individual opinion. The majority of concurring opinions became the Court's ruling. This process revealed each justice's thoughts on the case, but Marshall felt that it also undermined the Court's authority. By speaking with one voice, the Court could issue decisions that were definite and final. Of course, the majority would still rule, and justices in the minority were welcomed to issue a dissenting opinion, if they wished. However, beginning with the fall of 1801, a single "Opinion of the Court" would announce the justices' ruling in a case. It became a Supreme Court tradition that continues to this day.

Traditionally, the chief justice swears in newly elected presidents. Despite the animosity between them, Marshall and Thomas Jefferson observed this custom when it came time for Jefferson to take the oath of office. Both men understood that this ceremonial gesture would have special symbolic meaning for the nation. A Federalist judge would be swearing in a Democratic Republican president. As they stood solemnly at the podium of the Senate chamber, Jefferson raised his right hand and repeated the oath after Marshall. Together, they hoped this peaceful and patriotic transfer of power would help heal the country's deep political wounds.

Marshall and Jefferson were willing to place their personal differences aside for the nation's welfare. However, from this point forward they would be at odds over how America's government should function. Jefferson felt the Supreme Court should follow his lead as president, and issue rulings supporting his decisions. At the very least, Jefferson believed, the judiciary should stay out of the way of Congress and the president as they conducted the nation's business. Marshall, meanwhile, was working to establish the Court's independence. He believed the Supreme Court had final authority to interpret the Constitution. Sometimes that duty might cause the Court to rule on an action of the president or Congress.

In Marshall's view, if the president or Congress made a policy or law that violated the Constitution, then the Supreme Court could declare that policy or law void. This concept came to be known as judicial review. Thomas Jefferson, of course, strongly disagreed that the Court held any such power. Although nobody realized it at the time, a showdown was looming between the country's chief executive and its chief justice. The outcome would shape the federal government in ways that are still visible today.

# BUSHROD WASHINGTON: FRIEND AND COLLEAGUE

When John Marshall came to the Supreme Court in 1801, he made a point of personally getting to know each of his fellow justices. One member needed no introduction, however. It was Bushrod Washington, the first president's nephew. Marshall already knew Bushrod professionally, and the two men would become close friends during their twenty-nine years together on the Supreme Court.

They shared a common background, which no doubt helped cement their friendship. Like Marshall, Bushrod Washington had studied law at the College of William and Mary. They both went on to become successful Richmond attorneys, and they served together in the Virginia legislature. Their personal lives bore similarities too. John Marshall struggled with the declining mental and physical condition of his wife, Polly. Bushrod understood Marshall's pain; he too had a spouse in frail health.

A visible difference between the two men was their physical appearance. Marshall's build was tall, robust, and imposing, the opposite of Bushrod's narrow frame and small features. Unlike Marshall, who relished social gatherings, Bushrod was shy and reticent. He preferred the company of books, and spent so much time reading by dim light that he lost sight in one eye. Their political views matched closely, as did their understanding of the law. In nearly three decades together on the Supreme Court, John Marshall and Bushrod Washington disagreed on only three cases.

James Madison

would have to wait for someone from the Jefferson administration to deliver their paperwork.

Thomas Jefferson disliked how John Adams had rushed to fill so many judgeships before leaving office. Jefferson noted that all of Adams's appointees, including Marbury, were members of the Federalist Party. It was a blatant act of partisan politics, Jefferson felt. So when James Madison walked into his office with the undelivered commissions, Jefferson told Madison to keep them. By withholding the commissions, the new president figured he could foil his predecessor's plans to stock the courts with Federalist judges.

Nine months passed, and William Marbury rightly concluded that the Jefferson administration had no plans to give him his commission. Marbury's attorney appeared before the Supreme Court and asked for its assistance in the matter. In the Judiciary Act of 1789, Congress had given the Supreme Court the power to issue writs of mandamus. A writ of mandamus is a court order telling a public official to perform his or her duty. Marbury's attorney argued that, by withholding the commissions, James Madison was shirking his public duties. The attorney's request was unusual, but it did appear valid. Legally, his client seemed entitled to his commission. Before issuing a writ of mandamus, the justices decided to give James Madison an opportunity to explain. Marshall scheduled a hearing on the matter for the Court's next session.

When the Supreme Court reconvened in February 1803, Secretary of State Madison failed to appear for his hearing. On Jefferson's orders, he was ignoring the Court's authority. Jefferson contended that the Court had no right to tell an officer of the executive branch what to do. At this point, the justices could have easily issued the writ of mandamus ordering Madison to turn over Marbury's commission. But John Marshall viewed that option as unwise. Jefferson would almost certainly tell Madison to ignore the writ, leaving the Court looking ineffective and powerless. Yet to deny William Marbury's request would clearly be an injustice, for he had done nothing wrong. Marshall reexamined the facts of the case, searching for a third option that was both fair and enforceable.

On February 24, 1803, the justices assembled to announce their decision in *Marbury v. Madison*. One of them had taken ill, and to accommodate him they met in the living room of their boardinghouse rather than in the courtroom. By this point, the case had received considerable publicity. A crowd of curious onlookers packed the parlor, anxious to learn what might happen next in this confrontation between two branches of government. Marshall began to read the Court's ruling, which was unanimous. He would speak for nearly four hours. The lengthy opinion in *Marbury v. Madison* would go on to become a keystone of constitutional law, and one of the most frequently cited decisions in American legal history.

Marshall began by recognizing the difficulty and peculiarity of the case. He said that it boiled down to three basic questions: First, was William Marbury entitled to his commission? Second, if so, did the law offer him a remedy to obtain it? Third, if it did, would a writ of mandamus from the Supreme Court be the correct remedy? Marshall then proceeded to address each of these questions thoroughly and logically.

On the first point, Marshall said that Marbury was definitely entitled to his commission. The laws of the United States permitted President Adams to nominate any person he deemed worthy of the job, and Adams had chosen Marbury. The Senate then confirmed Marbury's appointment. Afterward, the president had signed the commission, and the secretary of state affixed to it the Great Seal of the United States. Every legal requirement in the process had been carefully fulfilled. Marshall concluded that there was absolutely no legitimate reason why Marbury should be denied his commission.

Marshall was quick to note that James Madison was not personally responsible for withholding the commission. As secretary of state, Madison was simply following the president's will, Marshall said. Having placed the responsibility squarely on Thomas Jefferson, Marshall condemned the government's behavior in this case. He accused the Jefferson administration of capriciously ignoring the law, much as a dictator might do. In a scathing insult, Marshall invoked the king of England, whose actions prior to American independence still stirred anger in 1803. Jefferson had behaved even more arbitrarily than that sovereign, Marshall said. "In Great Britain the king himself is sued in the respectful form of a petition, and he never fails to comply with the judgment of his court," Marshall pointed out.

Regarding the question of whether the law affords William Marbury a remedy, Marshall said that it must. "The very essence of civil liberty certainly consists in the right of every individual to claim the protection of the laws whenever he receives an injury. One of the first duties of government is to afford that protection," he explained.

Only the third and final question remained—whether a writ of mandamus from the Supreme Court was the appropriate remedy. Based on everything Marshall just said, it appeared that he was going to grant the writ. As the growing crowd of spectators looked on, he discussed the origins of the Court's authority. Marshall noted that the Constitution established the Supreme Court as the final decider of legal disputes. These disputes were supposed to begin in lower courts. If not satisfactorily resolved there, the parties involved had the right to appeal to a higher court. This appellate process could continue until the case reached the Supreme Court, where it would be decided once and for all.

Marshall methodically moved to his point: *Marbury v. Madison* did not begin in a lower court. William Marbury's attorney had taken the case directly to the Supreme Court. He did so because the Judiciary Act of 1789 authorized the Court to issue writs of mandamus as part of its original jurisdiction. However, the Constitution only permits a specific type of case to go directly to the Supreme Court, namely those "affecting Ambassadors, other public Ministers and Consuls, and those in which a State shall be a Party . . ." In other words, the Judiciary Act authorized a power not allowed by the Constitution. No act of Congress can violate the Constitution, Marshall said. Accordingly, the Judiciary Act of 1789 was unconstitutional. The Supreme Court had no authority to issue a writ of mandamus on behalf of William Marbury, even though the justices sympathized with his plight. The Constitution simply did not permit it.

With this complex ruling, John Marshall and his colleagues achieved an extraordinary legal precedent. They demonstrated the Supreme Court's ability to examine a law made by Congress, and declare that law void if it went against the Constitution. This was the principle of judicial review, and it was to become a fundamental and unique trait of the U.S. government. From this point forward, the Supreme Court would serve as the guardian of the Constitution, and both Congress and the president would be subject to its findings.

Thomas Jefferson despised the idea of judicial review, but he could do little to stop it. He had actually won the case of *Marbury v. Madison*.

An engraving depicting the portrait of George Washington by Gilbert Stuart

The Court did not order him to release William Marbury's commission, and he never did. Congress was also silent on the matter of judicial review. Marshall's logic was watertight, as usual. With this single case, the Supreme Court transformed itself from a floundering and ignored afterthought into an essential institution. It would maintain checks and balances on the other two branches of government, just as the Constitution's framers had intended.

The Supreme Court adjourned several days after handing down its decision in *Marbury v. Madison*, and John Marshall returned to Richmond for a much-needed respite. He required the solitude of home for his next undertaking, a project that would challenge him in new and unusual ways. He planned to write a book. It would be a biography of his late mentor, George Washington. Marshall's good friend, Bushrod Washington, had inherited his uncle's papers, files, and letters. The enormous collection of official and personal documents offered remarkable insight into the life of America's first president. Bushrod wanted to use them for a biography, but he personally was not up to the task due to his poor eyesight. Instead, he turned to Marshall.

The two friends reached an informal agreement. Bushrod would find a publisher for the book and furnish Marshall with all of his uncle's papers. Marshall would do the research and writing. They would split any profits equally. Marshall was excited about the project for two reasons. First, it would give him an opportunity to share the remarkable details of George Washington's life with ordinary citizens. Second, it would expand his abilities as a writer.

Marshall was already quite comfortable expressing himself in writing. As an attorney, politician, and judge, he had become accustomed to crafting long essays on complex subjects. But the Washington biography would be entirely different. He would need to sort through a lifetime of documents, culling vital details from a sea of minutiae. Then he would need to arrange that material into a story the average reader could understand and appreciate. The biography would run far longer than anything Marshall had written in the past. In fact, it was so lengthy that the publisher decided to release *The Life of George Washington* in five separate volumes. Together, the volumes would come to more than 3,200 pages. Marshall worked on the biography whenever his Supreme Court duties permitted. After five years, it was finally completed.

*The Life of George Washington* sold more than 7,000 copies, which at the time was a publishing success. The book became equally popular in Europe, where it was translated into several foreign languages. For the rest of his life, Marshall reworked and revised the biography, producing new and better editions of his work. He also wrote a shorter version intended specifically for young students. The biography is still prized today, not only for its masterful treatment of George Washington's life, but for the valuable insight it provides into the nation's early history.

In 1805, the Supreme Court faced a vexing and unusual distraction from its duties. One of its own justices had been placed on trial in the Senate, and was facing impeachment. Prosecutors accused the justice of inappropriate behavior in several cases over which he had presided on circuit court. (When the Supreme Court was not in session, each justice heard cases separately in lower courts.)

The judge in question was Samuel Chase of Baltimore, Maryland. Chase was in his mid-sixties and had served on the Supreme Court since 1796, when George Washington appointed him. Two decades before that, he was a powerful voice for the Revolution and a signer of the Declaration of Independence. A large and imposing man with a shock of white hair, Chase was known for his gifted legal mind, his outspoken opinions, and his remarkably short temper. Although John Marshall liked and admired Chase, the fiery Marylander often frustrated the chief justice with his disruptive outbursts.

Marshall rushed to the defense of his colleague. He knew that Chase too frequently gave in to his emotions, but at no time had his behavior approached grounds for impeachment. Marshall also feared the trial might set a dangerous precedent. If Congress could remove a Supreme Court justice for the most trivial of reasons, it would undermine the Court's independence. Marshall lined up witnesses for Chase's defense, and testified himself during the trial. To Marshall's relief, the Senate acquitted Chase of all charges. Although cleared of wrongdoing, the elder man had learned his lesson. For the rest of his career, Samuel Chase kept his emotions in check and observed proper decorum.

Samuel Chase

*John Marshall*

# JUSTICE AND CONTROVERSY

With its newly established authority of judicial review, the Supreme Court entered a hectic and productive era. A steady stream of important cases came before the justices, many of which would have far-reaching implications for the nation. At the same time, the Court itself was changing.

Supreme Court justices are entitled to remain on the bench their entire lives, although many eventually choose retirement. When a justice retires or dies, the president appoints a replacement. Thomas Jefferson had the opportunity to appoint three new justices during his time as president. In each instance, Jefferson searched for someone he felt would advance his Democratic Republican ideals, such as protecting states rights. John Marshall feared his old nemesis might simply choose hotheaded firebrands who would stir up trouble and sabotage the Court's effectiveness.

As it turned out, Jefferson's appointees were not narrow-minded radicals. Each favored calm, rational thought and political moderation. They also believed in an independent judiciary. These attitudes surprised and delighted Marshall. The three newcomers—William Johnson,

Brockholst Livingston, and Thomas Todd—added fresh viewpoints to the Supreme Court, and made it a stronger team. Todd joined the Court in 1807 not as a replacement, but because Congress had expanded the number of justices from six to seven. It was a reflection of the Court's growing workload. (Today's Supreme Court has nine judges.)

The intriguing case of *Fletcher v. Peck* came before the justices in 1810. Fletcher and Peck were two of countless real estate investors who became entangled in a notorious land scandal. The scandal dated back to 1795, when Georgia's legislature decided to sell a huge tract of state-owned land. Known as the Yazoo region, the land comprised 35 million acres in an area that would eventually comprise parts of Alabama and Mississippi. The land sale was a reckless act by corrupt politicians. Nearly every member of the Georgia legislature personally profited from it.

Georgia residents were outraged by the sale. The following year they voted out the corrupt politicians and elected a new legislature, which passed an act negating the land sale. But it was too late. The four New England real estate companies that bought the land had already sold it off in small parcels to scores of individuals. The state of Georgia persisted, claiming that it still owned the territory. If Georgia were permitted to renege on the sale, all those private citizens who bought parcels of land would lose their money. The fiasco triggered a wave of lawsuits, and *Fletcher v. Peck* was one of them.

In examining the case, the Supreme Court justices first considered the individual investor's plight. The original sale of land by corrupt politicians may certainly have been suspect, but the many private transactions that occurred afterward were not. People who bought land parcels from the New England firms had done nothing wrong. They had entered into a binding contract to purchase property in good faith from the property's legal owners. Those contracts were completely valid and legitimate. When Georgia's legislature reneged on the original land sale, it was also canceling out all the valid contracts that followed. John Marshall wondered if a state really had the power to do that. Perhaps it might, he said:

> were Georgia a single sovereign power. But Georgia cannot be viewed as a single, unconnected, sovereign power. . . . She is a part of a large empire; she is a member of the American union; and that union has a constitution, the supremacy of which all acknowledge, and which imposes limits to the legislatures of the several states . . . The Constitution of the United States declares that "no state shall pass any . . . law impairing the obligation of contracts."

In *Marbury v. Madison*, the Supreme Court found that a law of Congress was unconstitutional. In *Fletcher v. Peck*, the justices ruled that Georgia's law rescinding the land sale was unconstitutional. States were certainly entitled to govern themselves, but their laws could not supersede the Constitution. Advocates of states rights were not pleased, but private property owners applauded the ruling. It established that legitimate business transactions between individuals were protected by the Constitution.

The Supreme Court did not meet in 1811 due to lack of a quorum. A vacancy, the failing health of a senior member, and two absences meant that there were too few justices present to decide any cases. The two-year interlude made Marshall anxious to get the 1812 session underway. A backlog of cases had developed, and two new justices would be joining the Court. Marshall departed Richmond in January of 1812 for the trip back to Washington. Travel over the muddy Virginia roads was never easy, but heavy rains made this trip particularly hazardous. Marshall's stagecoach overturned, and he broke his collarbone. The chief justice arrived in Washington a week and a half late. Despite agonizing pain, he took his place on the bench and led the Court's proceedings.

Later that year, a national emergency overshadowed the normal bustle of activity in Washington. America and Great Britain were once again at war. The causes of the War of 1812 were many, including British attacks on U.S. shipping, and American designs on British territory in Canada. Ultimately, the conflict proved to be one that the United States was unprepared to fight. British troops marched on Washington in the summer of 1814, forcing the federal government to flee. The British set fire to the Capitol building and the White House, causing considerable damage, before finally withdrawing. The two nations reached a peace agreement later that year, and Marshall and his colleagues returned to

The president's mansion, now known as the White House, in Washington, D.C., after the British burned it during the War of 1812

their courtroom, only to find it virtually destroyed. For the next two years, the nation's highest court would be forced to meet in the modest Washington home of its clerk, Elias Caldwell.

By 1819, the Court was back in a formal setting and once again grappling with the states-rights controversy. Two decisions made during the 1819 term would further define the limits on state actions. The first was *Dartmouth College v. Woodward*. Dartmouth College, a private New Hampshire school, was established in 1769 and enjoyed a reputation as one of the nation's leading educational institutions. Like most colleges, its charter created a board of trustees, who oversaw the school's finances and managed its curriculum. Many of the school's trustees were Federalists, a fact that rankled New Hampshire's new Democratic-Republican governor. In 1816, he persuaded the legislature to pass a law making Dartmouth a state university under the governor's control. The governor appointed a new board of trustees, led by a man named William Woodward. Dartmouth sued, claiming the state had no right to meddle with its charter.

Daniel Webster, the celebrated New Hampshire orator and Dartmouth-trained attorney, argued before the Supreme Court on behalf of his alma mater. Webster eloquently captured the essence of the case. It was about much more than a single school's right to remain independent, he said. It was about a state government's seizure of private property. "It is, in some sense, the case of every man among us who has property of which he may be stripped," Webster noted. "For the question is simply this: Shall our State Legislatures be allowed to take that which is not their own, to turn it from its original use, and apply it to such ends or purposes as they, in their discretion, shall see fit!"

The justices agreed with Webster's impassioned plea. The New Hampshire legislature had acted inappropriately, they ruled. Dartmouth's charter was a contract, and therefore was protected by the "contract clause" of the Constitution. Dartmouth would remain private and independent. The same clause that had preserved the rights of land buyers in Georgia now saved a tiny college some 1,200 miles to the north. In the future, the Constitution's contract clause would be invoked repeatedly to protect private property and business from government intrusion.

The second major case of 1819 clarified the relationship between state governments and the federal government. *McCulloch v. Maryland* pitted the state of Maryland against the Bank of the United States. State governments typically established—or chartered—banks, but the U.S. Bank was a federal institution that had been chartered by Congress. Its purpose was to help the federal government manage America's economy. Most states disliked the U.S. Bank, since it assumed some of the control they previously held over their own individual economies. Some states began looking for ways to fight the U.S. Bank and cripple its activities. Maryland did so by levying a heavy tax against the bank's branch office in Baltimore.

Branch manager James McCulloch refused to pay the Maryland tax, so state authorities pressed charges and had him convicted in court. McCulloch appealed his case all the way to the Supreme Court. Daniel Webster once again stood before the Court, this time as McCulloch's lawyer. Attorney General William Wirt also joined the cause on behalf of the Bank of the United States. The state of Maryland sent its best lawyers to oppose them. Typically, the Court allowed only three days for attorneys from both sides to make their case. Given the complexity and weight of this case, arguments were permitted to continue for nine days.

Maryland's attorneys called the U.S. Bank unconstitutional, since the Constitution never specifically authorized Congress to charter banks. They also talked at length about a state's right to raise revenue through taxation, but Marshall and the other justices were unconvinced. That right was not absolute, they said. In announcing the Court's opinion on March 6, 1819, Marshall pointed out:

> If the states may tax one instrument employed by the government in the execution of its powers, they may tax any and every other instrument. They may tax the mail; they may tax the mint; they may tax patent rights . . . they may tax all the means employed by the government, to an excess which would defeat all the ends of government. This was not intended by the American people. They did not design to make their government dependent on the states.

The Court's decision was unanimous. Marshall and his colleagues

The United States Bank in Philadelphia, Pennsylvania, circa 1830

Engraving depicting a ship loaded with slaves

noted that the Constitution charges Congress with regulating the nation's commerce. A bank is certainly a reasonable tool for carrying out that duty, they said, even if the Constitution does not specifically mention it. Since states may not levy taxes on the federal government or its operations, Maryland's tax on the U.S. Bank was unconstitutional.

The ruling was a slap in the face of states rights supporters, and they knew it. For months afterward, essays and letters criticizing the decision poured into newspapers, where editors happily published them. *McCulloch v. Maryland* had struck a raw nerve, especially in the South, where states rights were considered virtually sacred. In the South, the issue of states rights was tied inextricably to the right to own slaves. Southern plantation owners did not want a federal government powerful enough to outlaw slavery, ruining their livelihood in the process. Some of the sharpest criticism of the McCulloch decision came from John Marshall's native state of Virginia.

The issue of slavery never came before Marshall during his time on the Supreme Court, but it is clear that he opposed it. The Court once heard an international maritime case involving a Venezuelan smuggling ship filled with enslaved Africans. Marshall took the opportunity to castigate slavery: "That every man has a natural right to the fruits of his own labor, is generally admitted; and that no other person can rightfully deprive him of those fruits, and appropriate them against his will, seems to be the necessary result of this admission," he wrote in the Court's ruling.

In later years, Marshall became active in groups that helped freed slaves return to Africa. He bemoaned the divisive effect that slavery had on America, and hoped the matter could someday be resolved peacefully. Marshall would not live to see the war that the North and South would fight over slavery and their other differences.

# Marshall's Appalachian Adventure

Virginians never stopped thinking of John Marshall as one of their own. They sought out his help when needed, and he always complied. During the War of 1812, when a British invasion of Richmond seemed possible, local officials asked Marshall to help organize the city's defenses. The chief justice seriously doubted Richmond's ability to repel a British assault. Regardless, he dutifully drilled young volunteers into militiamen, just as he had done during the Revolutionary War.

The attack on Richmond never came, but in late 1812 Marshall's native state called on him once more. Virginia's western half was still wild and largely inaccessible, and the state legislature hoped to improve travel through the region. Good roads and waterways would open up the wilderness to more commerce and settlement. The first step was to send a survey party through the mountainous terrain to identify the best land and water routes. The legislature asked Supreme Court chief justice John Marshall, now fifty-seven years old, to lead the survey team.

Marshall gladly accepted. He had grown up in the wilderness, and the chance to return to it thrilled him. For a few weeks, he would be able to forget about the courtroom and Washington politics, and once again become a frontiersman. Marshall set out with his team of nearly two dozen surveyors on September 1, 1812. They slowly made their way westward through the Appalachian Mountains, navigating by boat whenever possible. Marshall made detailed notes about water depth and land elevation as they passed through 250 miles of pristine woodlands. The weather was warm and dry, making the journey exceptionally pleasant.

Upon returning six weeks later, Marshall wrote his report to the legislature. With the same clarity and insight of a Supreme Court ruling, he described potential passages through the Appalachians. It seemed possible to establish a link with the Ohio River on the other side, Marshall concluded, and from there on to the Mississippi. Virginia's legislature was delighted, and eventually implemented his suggestions for trans-Appalachian travel.

James Monroe, fifth president of the United States

# GOLDEN YEARS

**B**y 1824, John Marshall was beginning to feel the effects of age. Now sixty-nine, his mind remained sharper than ever, and he walked regularly to stay in shape, but his vitality was fading. One icy February evening in Washington, he slipped while stepping from a stagecoach and hit his head, knocking himself unconscious. The fall did no permanent damage, and he was alert after a few moments, but it dislocated his shoulder. The embarrassing incident also bruised his ego.

"Old men do not get over sprains and hurts as quickly as young ones," he grumbled in a letter to his wife Polly. "Although I feel no pain when perfectly still, yet I cannot get up and move about without difficulty, and cannot put on my coat. Of course, I cannot go to Court." After nearly a quarter century, Marshall had become a welcomed fixture in Washington, and a steady flow of visitors lifted his spirits. He mentioned to Polly with obvious pride that President James Monroe had recently stopped by with warm wishes for a speedy recovery. Some visitors brought cakes and jellies to sustain the chief justice as he healed.

The steamboat made it possible to travel without the aid of the wind and to move upstream.

Within two weeks, Marshall was back at work. The clamor over states rights continued unabated, and time was precious. Another landmark case was before the Court, this time involving a dispute with the state of New York. On the Court's docket it appeared officially as *Gibbons v. Ogden*, but newspaper reporters dubbed it the Great Steamboat Case. A relatively new invention, the steamboat was rapidly becoming America's preferred mode of transportation. Captains no longer needed to rely on a steady breeze to propel their craft. Steam-powered engines offered continuous, reliable propulsion, and could chug upriver against the strongest current.

Steamboat companies began popping up across the country. They courted state legislatures for the exclusive right to operate their steamboats within state waters. One company successfully negotiated a contract with New York. The state legislature decreed that only steamboats owned by that company could operate in New York waters. All others were banned. This monopoly angered the neighboring states of New Jersey and Connecticut. They declared that steamboats licensed by New York were banned from their waters. As the feud worsened, states warned that they would seize any steamboat caught violating their ban. By awarding a monopoly, New York had inadvertently hamstrung interstate commerce. Steamboats bottled up inside their home waters were unable to deliver cargo to out-of-state destinations. A flurry of lawsuits hit the courts, with *Gibbons v. Ogden* going all the way to the highest court.

Marshall and his fellow justices concluded that the case turned on a single question: are states entitled to pass laws restricting interstate commerce? Marshall freely acknowledged that states must sometimes impose regulations affecting business. Safety inspections and health laws were good examples, he said. Requiring private industry to observe those rules no doubt slowed the trade of goods. But those laws existed for another reason, namely public safety. The effect on business was purely coincidental. However, New York's legislature was not protecting the public's health or safety when it awarded the steamboat monopoly. It was arbitrarily restricting commerce.

Marshall further noted that the Constitution specifically gives Congress—not the states—power to regulate foreign and interstate commerce. The Constitution's framers knew from bitter experience that, when left to the states, the result was a confusing patchwork of conflicting laws and regulations. Disputes inevitably arose, just as they had with the New York steamboat monopoly, and everyone suffered as business slowed to a halt. Federal control avoids that quagmire. While some states may disagree with a federal commerce law, at least that law applies consistently across the entire nation. The states must then hash out their dispute with Congress, not each other, and as a result interstate commerce proceeds. As for the Great Steamboat Case, Marshall pointed out that any vessel with a federal coasting license is authorized to navigate freely throughout the United States, including the waters of

New York. Accordingly, he said, the monopoly awarded by New York's legislature was void.

Unlike other cases involving states rights, the Supreme Court ruling in *Gibbons v. Ogden* stirred no controversy. People disliked unfair and troublesome monopolies, and they recognized the value of free trade. Even New Yorkers could not complain too loudly. Once the state's steamboat restrictions were lifted, New York City rapidly grew into the heart of American commerce. For John Marshall, all the talk about steamboats had piqued his curiosity. When the Court's session ended, he climbed aboard one for the trip back to Richmond.

At home, the chief justice spent most of his time busily revising his George Washington biography or working on some other project. A small outbuilding stood in one corner of his yard, and Marshall converted it into an office. Visitors who came knocking on the main house's front door were sent around back to the tiny brick structure, where they typically found Marshall hard at work. By this time, most people were writing with steel pens, but the chief justice still preferred the feel of a quill in his hand. The feather instrument harkened back to America's colonial days, perhaps reminding him of his youth. Despite his hectic work schedule, Marshall was never too busy to greet guests. Acquaintances during this time universally described him as plain, pleasant, and mannerly.

Marshall knew that time was catching up with him. Many of his friends and colleagues had already passed on, and so too had his sole nemesis. Thomas Jefferson died on July 4, 1826. Marshall helped organize Richmond's day of mourning for the former president and author of the Declaration of Independence. He and Jefferson were lifelong adversaries, but had worked toward the same goal—a stronger and better America. Marshall respected Jefferson's enormous contributions to the nation, even if he disliked the man personally.

In the fall of 1829, Marshall found himself standing in a familiar place from the past. Nearly half a century earlier, he had launched his political career by winning a seat in the Virginia House of Delegates. Now he was back in the chamber of that legislative body. Virginians had decided to update their state constitution, which dated all the way back to 1776, and they wanted the benefit of John Marshall's wisdom. The chief justice initially declined when asked to participate in the state constitutional convention. At seventy-four, he felt he no longer had the energy, but his admirers insisted. Marshall reluctantly agreed and assumed the role of delegate for a final time. As expected, he brought a remarkable breadth of understanding and insight to the state convention. Marshall drafted the new constitution's judicial section, and his fellow delegates changed hardly a word before approving it.

His duty to Virginia complete, Marshall traveled to Washington for the next session of the Supreme Court. The tightly knit team he had assembled decades earlier was now gone, and so were the long streaks of unanimous opinions. Not all of the justices lodged together, as had been the custom previously. Some of the newer appointees brought their families to Washington, and preferred to stay with them. Without the informal dinnertime discussions of the past, Marshall found it harder to build a consensus. The Court became more fractious, and its decisions were often sharply split. The chief justice longed for the days of harmonious teamwork. In 1831, he confided to a friend that he was contemplating retirement.

Later that year, Marshall encountered the first serious health problem of his life. Doctors diagnosed the source of his pain as bladder stones, and he journeyed to Philadelphia for an operation. The procedure required a small abdominal incision through which the surgeon inserted forceps to grab and remove the stones. Modern anesthesia was not yet available, meaning Marshall had to endure the surgery fully awake and in pain. Remarkably, his surgeon found and extracted more than a thousand of the tiny stones. Marshall survived the harrowing ordeal and made a full recovery.

The next hardship would take a far greater toll on him. His beloved wife, Polly, had been in poor health for many years, and her condition was rapidly deteriorating. Marshall set aside his work to care for Polly, and was with her constantly during her final days in December 1831. Her death was a crushing blow, and one from which he would never totally recover. Still grieving months later, he told a colleague that he shed tears for Polly nearly every night before falling asleep.

Marshall's tenure on the Supreme Court was nearing its end, but he would have one more grand opportunity to defend the Constitution and protect the rights that it promises. The chief justice had long been sympathetic to the plight of Native Americans. Since before he was born, white settlers had been encroaching on tribal lands and pushing

An illustration of a Native American lying in ambush.

out its inhabitants. The Native Americans tried to defend themselves and their property in a variety of ways, some peaceful and some violent, but with little success. White settlers kept coming, taking land that did not belong to them.

Native American tribes began negotiating with state governments, hoping to preserve the fraction of their territory that still remained. The treaties that resulted were patently unfair, but at least they promised a measure of protection under white law. However, state governments were notoriously lax in honoring the treaties. They failed to restrain settlers from encroaching upon tribal ground, and when a previously signed treaty became inconvenient, they simply canceled it. This was the case with the state of Georgia, which previously agreed to preserve territory of the Cherokee Nation. Georgia changed its mind in the late 1820s after gold was discovered on Cherokee ground. It promptly revoked the treaty, and claimed the tribal territory for itself.

John Marshall abhorred Georgia's underhanded behavior, but could do nothing to stop it. The bewildered Cherokees appealed to the Supreme Court, but the justices were unable to help them. Since the Cherokee Nation did not qualify as a foreign country, it had no legal standing to be heard by the Court. "If courts were permitted to indulge their sympathies, a case better calculated to excite them can scarcely be imagined," Marshall lamented. "A people once numerous, powerful, and truly independent, found by our ancestors in the quiet and uncontrolled possession of an ample domain . . . have yielded their lands by successive treaties. . . ." As with slavery, Marshall and his colleagues could not issue a direct ruling on the matter, but they were making their displeasure known.

In 1832, fortune presented the justices with an opportunity to finally rule on Georgia's actions against the Cherokees. A case came before the Court involving a New England minister named Samuel Worcester, who was arrested for trespassing on Cherokee land. Worcester explained that he was performing missionary work, and that he held a federal permit entitling him to do so. However, Georgia's laws establishing its domain over Cherokee territory said that Worcester needed a state permit to be there. A Georgia court found him guilty of violating state law and sentenced him to four years in prison. The minister appealed his conviction to the Supreme Court.

When *Worcester v. Georgia* appeared on the Court's docket, Marshall knew he had the opening he needed to assist the Cherokees. He began by addressing Georgia's conviction of Samuel Worcester. A state had no right to arrest an individual for performing work authorized by the federal government, Marshall said. He overturned Georgia's conviction and ordered Worcester released. The decision added fuel to the raging states-rights controversy, but there was more to come. Marshall next turned to the state laws enabling Georgia to seize tribal land. He criticized "the system of legislation lately adopted by the legislature of Georgia, in relation to the Cherokee nation," and said it was "repugnant to the Constitution, laws, and treaties of the United States." The Supreme Court struck down Georgia's Cherokee land laws.

The ruling was not unanimous, nor would it reverse the plight of Native Americans, but the justices had gone on record: The states, and ultimately the federal government, were treating America's indigenous peoples unfairly. In the Court's view, it was a disgrace to the wording and spirit of the Constitution. *Worcester v. Georgia* would mark the last great ruling of John Marshall's career. His final three years as chief justice would be largely uneventful, and the thought of retirement grew ever more appealing.

On a warm spring morning in 1835, Marshall was walking to a cemetery outside of Richmond. The Court was in recess, and he was making a routine visit to Polly's grave. Suddenly, the seventy-nine-year-old chief justice grew weak and collapsed. Two strangers helped him home, and immediately he made plans to be seen by his surgeon in Philadelphia. The prognosis was not at all good. Marshall was suffering from an enlarged liver, and his doctor could do nothing to help him. In the weeks that followed, his appetite diminished and he rapidly lost weight and energy. His mind was still sharp, but his body was wasting away. Marshall's oldest son, Thomas, set out from his Virginia farm, hoping to arrive in Philadelphia before it was too late.

In a sad and ironic twist of fate, Marshall ended up outliving his son. Thomas died in a freak accident while passing through the city of Baltimore. A brick chimney collapsed after being struck by lightning, falling on Thomas and killing him instantly. Marshall's caregivers decided not to inform him of his son's death. The chief justice was now in his final days, and they saw no reason to put him through the mental anguish.

United States Supreme Court chief justice John Marshall died on Monday, July 6, 1835. His body was taken to Richmond, where he was laid to rest next to Polly. The nation that mourned John Marshall's death was remarkably different from the one of his birth. The British colonies had banded together and won a hard-fought independence. Following a rocky start, they successfully evolved into a unified nation, one that was flourishing economically and rapidly growing westward. The U.S. Constitution, almost half a century old when Marshall died, had provided a solid foundation for prosperity. An elegant statement of freedom, balance, and fairness, the Constitution would go on to become one of humanity's most celebrated documents. Countries around the world would use it as a template for their own constitution. John Marshall's vigorous defense of the Constitution helped cement its success. During

The statue of John Marshall at the Philadelphia Museum of Art

his thirty-four years as Supreme Court leader, Marshall ensured that presidents, Congress, and the states all obeyed the language and spirit of America's supreme set of laws. Without his unyielding determination, the Constitution may not have attained its lofty place in American government and culture.

As chief justice, Marshall helped decide more than a thousand cases, authoring the Court's opinion in roughly half of them. He administered the oath of office to five different presidents. Before that, he fought in the American Revolution and was a friend to George Washington. Marshall was also a lawyer, legislator, diplomat, and cabinet officer. He led others with his example, he built consensus through good-natured debate, and he showed equal respect for friend and foe. John Adams, reflecting back on his presidency once remarked, "My gift of John Marshall to the people of the United States was the proudest act of my life."

# Remembering Marshall

Tributes to Chief Justice John Marshall can be found across the United States. Marshall University in Huntington, West Virginia, is named after him, as are four law schools located in Virginia, Ohio, Georgia, and Illinois. Franklin & Marshall College in Lancaster, Pennsylvania, honors both the chief justice and Benjamin Franklin. Dozens of high schools, counties, and communities across the nation also bear the Marshall name.

The federal government has honored Marshall in the past by placing his image on paper money and postal stamps. In Washington, D.C., a bronze statue of him graces the ground floor of the Supreme Court building, as does one at Marshall Park on Constitution Avenue. The Philadelphia Museum of Art also maintains a likeness of the chief justice. In 1998, Marshall University unveiled an eight-foot bronze statue of him on the grounds of its library. John Marshall's home in Richmond, Virginia, is now a well-maintained museum, complete with furnishings and artifacts from his life.

# APPENDIX
## SELECTED CONSTITUTIONAL CASES

| *Marbury v. Madison* (1803) ||
|---|---|
| **PLAINTIFF** | **DEFENDANT** |
| William Marbury petitioned the Supreme Court to force Madison to release a document he needed. | U.S. Secretary of State James Madison refused to turn over Marbury's document. |
| **Arguments** ||
| The Judiciary Act of 1789 authorized the Court to issue writs of mandamus, ordering public officials to do their duty. | As an officer of the executive branch, it was Madison's prerogative to withhold the document. |
| **Decision** ||
| The Constitution does not permit the Supreme Court to issue writs of mandamus. The Judiciary Act of 1789 was unconstitutional. ||

## Fletcher v. Peck (1810)

| PLAINTIFF | DEFENDANT |
|---|---|
| Robert Fletcher claimed Peck sold him land he did not truly own. | John Peck purchased the land from its rightful owner at the time. |

### Arguments

| | |
|---|---|
| Georgia's legislature revoked its original land sale. | Peck bought and sold the land in good faith. |

### Decision

The Constitution prohibited Georgia from voiding land transfer contracts, even though the original sale may have been made by corrupt legislators.

## Dartmouth College v. Woodward (1819)

| PLAINTIFF | DEFENDANT |
|---|---|
| Dartmouth wished to remain a private institution, so it sued to stop the state of New Hampshire from taking control of it. | State appointee William Woodward sought to take control of Dartmouth, as authorized by the New Hampshire legislature. |

### Arguments

| | |
|---|---|
| The school's private charter prevented the state from turning it into a public institution. | The state had the right to amend the school's charter. |

### Decision

The school's charter is a contract, and the Constitution says that no state shall make any law impairing the obligation of contracts.

## McCulloch v. Maryland (1819)

| PLAINTIFF | DEFENDANT |
|---|---|
| James McCulloch, head of the Baltimore branch of the U.S. Bank, said that Maryland had no right to tax a federal bank. | The state of Maryland contended that the U.S. Bank was not a legitimate instrument of the federal government. |

### Arguments

| | |
|---|---|
| No state may interfere with the operations of the federal government. | The Constitution does not authorize Congress to charter banks. |

### Decision

A bank is a proper and suitable instrument to assist the federal government in collecting and disbursing revenue. Since federal laws have supremacy over state laws, Maryland had no power to interfere with the bank's operation by taxing it.

## Cohens v. Virginia (1821)

| PLAINTIFF | DEFENDANT |
|---|---|
| Philip and Mendes Cohen were convicted for selling lottery tickets in Virginia. | Virginia law banned the sale of out-of-state lottery tickets within its borders. |

### Arguments

| | |
|---|---|
| The lottery ticket sales were authorized by an act of Congress. | The Constitution's Eleventh Amendment precluded the Supreme Court from hearing the case. |

### Decision

The Supreme Court is the final arbiter of the Constitution, and the Eleventh Amendment does not prevent it from deciding a legitimate federal question.

## Gibbons v. Ogden (1824)

| PLAINTIFF | DEFENDANT |
|---|---|
| Thomas Gibbons sued because New York law prevented his steamboats from sailing in its waters. | Aaron Ogden held a New York state license for operating steamboats. |

### Arguments

| | |
|---|---|
| Gibbons' federal coasting license allowed him to operate his steamboats in New York | New York was entitled to regulate the navigation of its waters. |

### Decision

The Constitution prohibits states from interfering with the power of Congress to regulate interstate commerce.

## Worcester v. Georgia (1832)

| PLAINTIFF | DEFENDANT |
|---|---|
| Samuel Worcester was convicted of living in Cherokee territory without a Georgia license. | Georgia claimed dominion over the Cherokee territory. |

### Arguments

| | |
|---|---|
| Congress authorized Worcester's missionary work among the Cherokees. | Georgia's legislature was entitled to restrict residency within the territory. |

### Decision

The Constitution grants Congress sole authority to regulate relations with sovereign entities. Accordingly, states could not redraw the boundaries of Native American lands or forbid residence in those territories.

## Barron v. Baltimore (1833)

| PLAINTIFF | DEFENDANT |
|---|---|
| John Barron sued the city of Baltimore for making the water around his wharf too shallow for boat use by diverting the streams that fed it. | Baltimore city workers diverted the flow of streams while engaging in street construction. |

### Arguments

| | |
|---|---|
| The Fifth Amendment prohibits the government from taking private property without just compensation. | The Fifth Amendment was not applicable to this case. |

### Decision

The Constitution's first ten amendments (also known as the Bill of Rights) restrain only the federal government, not state or local governments.

Old Main, the oldest building on the campus of Marshall University in Huntington, West Virginia

# TIMELINE

**1755**    Born on September 24, in Germanton (now Midland), in Fauquier County, Virginia.

**1775**    Serves as lieutenant in Continental Army during the American Revolutionary War.

**1780**    Studies law under jurist George Wythe at William and Mary College; admitted to Virginia bar.

**1782**    Wins a seat in the Virginia House of Delegates.

**1783**    Marries Mary Willis "Polly" Ambler.

**1784**    First child, Thomas, born.

**1787**    Reelected to Virginia House of Delegates.

**1795**    Reelected to Virginia House of Delegates.

**1797**    Sent on diplomatic mission to France by President John Adams.

**1799**    Elected to U.S. House of Representatives.

**1800**    Appointed secretary of state.

**1801**    Appointed chief justice of the U.S. Supreme Court by President Adams.

**1805 -1807**    Publishes a five-volume biography on the life of George Washington.

**1812**    Leads a team of nearly two dozen surveyors through western Virginia.

**1829**    Serves as member of the Virginia convention to update the state's constitution.

**1831**    Wife, Polly, dies.

**1835**    Dies on July 6.

# Sources

**CHAPTER ONE:**
DEFENDER OF THE CONSTITUTION

p. 11    "The jury have now heard . . ." David Robertson, *Reports of the Trials of Colonel Aaron Burr* (Philadelphia: Hopkins and Earle, 1808), 445.

p. 15    "So great is his sophistry . . ." Jean Edward Smith, *John Marshall: Definer of a Nation* (New York: Henry Holt and Company, 1996), 12.

**CHAPTER TWO:**
LESSONS IN LIFE AND LAW

p. 22-23    "He was an excellent companion . . ." Smith, *John Marshall*, 64.

**CHAPTER THREE:**
LAWYER AND LEADER

p. 31    "be submitted to a convention . . ." Smith, *John Marshall*, 114.

**CHAPTER FOUR:**
MISSION TO FRANCE

p. 44    "My clients would know . . ." Smith, *John Marshall*, 185.

p. 51    "they are calculated to create . . ." Ibid., 244.

**CHAPTER FIVE:**
IN SERVICE OF THE NATION

p. 57    "When I waited on the . . ." Smith, *John Marshall*, 14.

## CHAPTER SIX:
### MARBURY V. MADISON

p. 66        "In Great Britain the king . . ." John Marshall, *The Writings of John Marshall, Late Chief Justice of the United States, Upon the Federal Constitution* (Boston: James Munroe and Company, 1839), 11.

p. 66-67    "The very essence of . . ." Ibid., 11.

## CHAPTER SEVEN:
### JUSTICE AND CONTROVERSY

p. 75        "were Georgia a single sovereign . . ." Marshall, *Writings of John Marshall*, 135.

p. 77        "It is, in some sense . . ." Samuel Gilman Brown, *The Works of Rufus Choate with a Memoir of his Life* (Boston: Little, Brown and Company, 1862), 516.

p. 78        "If the states may tax . . ." Marshall, *Writings of John Marshall*, 184.

p. 81        "That every man has a . . ." Smith, *John Marshall*, 487.

## CHAPTER EIGHT:
### GOLDEN YEARS

p. 85        "Old men do not . . ." Smith, *John Marshall*, 476.

p. 91        "If courts were permitted to . . ." Marshall, *Writings of John Marshall*, 412.

p. 92        "the system of legislation . . ." Ibid., 447.

p. 94        "My gift of John Marshall . . ." Charles Warren, *The Supreme Court in United States History, Vol. 1* (Boston: Little, Brown and Company, 1922), 178.

# BIBLIOGRAPHY

Hobson, Charles F. *The Great Chief Justice: John Marshall and the Rule of Law*. Lawrence, Kan.: University Press of Kansas, 2000.

Marshall, John. *The Writings of John Marshall, Late Chief Justice of the United States, Upon the Federal Constitution*. Boston: James Munroe and Company, 1839.

Newmyer, R. Kent. *John Marshall and the Heroic Age of the Supreme Court*. Baton Rouge, La.: Louisiana State University Press, 2007.

Robertson, David. *Reports of the Trials of Colonel Aaron Burr*. Philadelphia: Hopkins and Earle, 1808.

Simon, James F. *What Kind of Nation: Thomas Jefferson, John Marshall, and the Epic Struggle to Create a United States*. New York: Simon & Schuster, 2002.

Sloan, Cliff, and David McKean. *The Great Decision: Jefferson, Adams, Marshall, and the Battle for the Supreme Court*. New York: PublicAffairs, 2009.

Smith, Jean Edward. *John Marshall: Definer of a Nation*. New York: Henry Holt and Company, 1996.

Warren, Charles. *The Supreme Court in United States History, Vol. 1*. Boston: Little, Brown and Company, 1922.

# WEB SITES

HTTP://WWW.LVA.VIRGINIA.GOV/EXHIBITS/
MARSHALL/

Read this brief but fascinating profile of John Marshall, presented by the Library of Virginia.

HTTP://WWW.PRESERVATIONVIRGINIA.ORG/
MARSHALL/INDEX.HTML

Take an online tour of John Marshall's home, which is now a museum operated by the non-profit group Preservation Virginia.

HTTP://HISTORY.STATE.GOV/MILESTONES/1784-1800/
XYZ

Find out more about the international incident known as the XYZ Affair, in which John Marshall played a pivotal role.

HTTP://WWW.SUPREMECOURT.GOV/ABOUT/PHOTO14.
ASPX

This page from the Supreme Court's Web site shows the Old Supreme Court Chamber inside the U.S. Capitol. John Marshall heard many important cases here.

HTTP://WWW.OURDOCUMENTS.GOV/DOC.
PHP?FLASH=OLD&DOC=19

View an actual, handwritten document from the landmark Supreme Court case *Marbury v. Madison*, courtesy of the National Archives.

HTTP://WWW.JOHNMARSHALLFOUNDATION.ORG/

The John Marshall Foundation maintains an extensive online library covering the life and times of the great chief justice.

# INDEX

treason, 9–11

U. S. Bank, 78, *79,* 81
U. S. Capitol, *54–55,* 56, 76
U. S. Congress, 13, 31, 63, 67–68, 78, 81, 87
U. S. Constitution, 10, 12–13, *30,* 31, 33–34, 49–50, 57,
    60, 67–68, 78, 87
U. S. Department of State, 54–55
U. S. Supreme Court, 12–13, 57–60, 63, 65–68, 73

Valley Forge, Pennsylvania, *21,* 22–23
Virginia House of Delegates, 25, 29, 31, 88
von Steuben, Friedrich Wilhelm, 23

War of 1812, 76, 82
Washington, Bushrod, 49–50, 61, 69
Washington, D. C., 56
Washington, George, 14, *21,* 21–22, 27, 36, *36,* 41, 44,
    49, *68,* 69–70, 88, 94
Webster, Daniel, 77–78
White House, the, 56, *76*
Wirt, William, 78
Worcester, Samuel, 91–92
*Worcester v. Georgia,* 91–92
writs of mandamus, 65–67
Wythe, George, 25

XYZ Affair, 49, 55

# CREDITS